The Kids' Holiday Book

by Ed and Roon Frost
illustrated by Carol Leach

Just for Kids
P.O. Box 1602
Portsmouth, NH 03802

Ed Frost has been writing and editing professionally, since he was an under-graduate at Stanford University. After years as an award-winning film producer, he began to create travel guides with his wife. *The Kids Holiday Book* is his second children's book.

A freelance writer for 15 years, Roon Frost has seen her byline in a wide range of national and regional publications from AMERICANA to THE WASHINGTON POST. Her first book, *The Little Boy Book,* continues to draw praise from child-care specialists, parents, and teachers. The Frosts live in Eliot, ME with their son.

Artist Carol Leach, a resident of Kittery, ME, has her own line of greeting cards for kids and sew-your-own dolls. An elementary-school teacher for almost ten years, she has illustrated books, consulted for a children's museum, and worked as a juvenile bookstore manager.

Ligature Typography, quality advertising and book typographers of Portsmouth, NH, set the type.

Printing is by McNaughton & Gunn, Ann Arbor, MI.

This book could not have been completed without the advice and assistance of many people. Special thanks to:
• Rabbi David Mark of Portsmouth's Temple Israel for his help with Jewish holidays;
• B.T. Batsford, Ltd. of London, England for permission to print the map on page 99;
• Cathy Goodwin and the youngsters at Eliot's Kid Care for their honest "grading" of our activities—and to all the children everywhere who keep us thinking.

FIRST EDITION

ISBN 0-9618806-3-5

To order, contact:
   Independent Publishers Group
   814 North Franklin Street
   Chicago, IL 60610
   1-800/888-4741
Please include $3 for postage and handling.

TABLE OF CONTENTS

TIME

To have the most fun with this book, it helps to know a little bit about time.

How old are you?

If you are 7 years old, that means you have lived ___ units of time that we call a year.

When you are young, a year can seem like a very long time. But not when there are lots of holidays and special days to celebrate!

Circle the things people use to help tell time.

A YEAR IN TIME

A year is the time it takes our planet, earth, to circle once around the star we call the sun.

Earth spins, like a top, as it orbits the sun. When it has gone around the sun once completely, we say another year has passed.

Did you know?

As earth orbits the sun, it moves more than twice as fast as an Apollo rocket. But we never feel it moving!

Most people do feel a change in the seasons, though. What are the warm seasons where you live?

Do you have a yo-yo? If you unwind it slowly, then spin it around your head, you'll have an idea of what earth does in orbit.

What keeps earth in orbit? (Hint: Gravity works a little like an invisible string.)

SEASONS and the TILT of the EARTH

Take a knitting needle and stick it straight through an orange. Tilt the knitting needle a little. The earth tilts much like this, as it spins in orbit around the sun. This tilt creates our seasons.

Do you see four seasons, or four different places earth can be in its orbit around the sun?

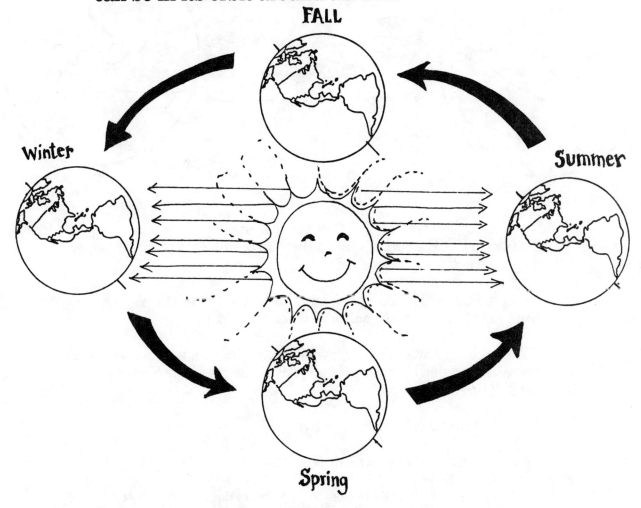

Winter, spring, summer, fall = 1 year.

The Sun's Rays

The seasons are different, depending where you live. When the top half of the earth tips *away* from the sun, it grows *cooler* there. Fall and winter are the chilly seasons in the northern part of the earth. But the bottom half of earth gets warmer in those seasons. Do you think that's because this part of the earth is tilting toward the sun?

WINTER   SUMMER   SUN'S RAYS

Did you know?

The top half of the earth is called the Northern Hemisphere. What do you think the bottom half is called?

Can you find the United States and Canada in the picture of earth? Do we live in the top half or the bottom half of our earth?

(When the top half of the earth tips *toward* the sun, it grows *warm* again there. Spring and summer are the warm seasons in the Northern Hemisphere.)

Which is your favorite season? Why?

equator = imaginary line that divides earth into north and south (or two hemispheres.)

hemisphere = half of the earth from the equator to the very top, or bottom.

pole = the farthest anyone can go, north or south; the top or bottom of earth.

SUMMER ～ WINTER

If you live in the northern half of the earth, do you
know which way the earth is tilting in the different
seasons?

Write the letter that shows which way the earth is tilting in the different
seasons.　　T = toward the sun　　A = away from the sun

(INDIAN MOON SIGNS (

Many early peoples used the moon, as well as the sun, to tell time. The American Indians (or Native Americans), the Chinese, and the Hebrews (as early Jews are known) divided their years into moons.

How many moons are there in a year?

Can you guess what the Woodland Indians called each moon by the symbols below? If you unscramble the words, you'll know whether you guessed correctly.

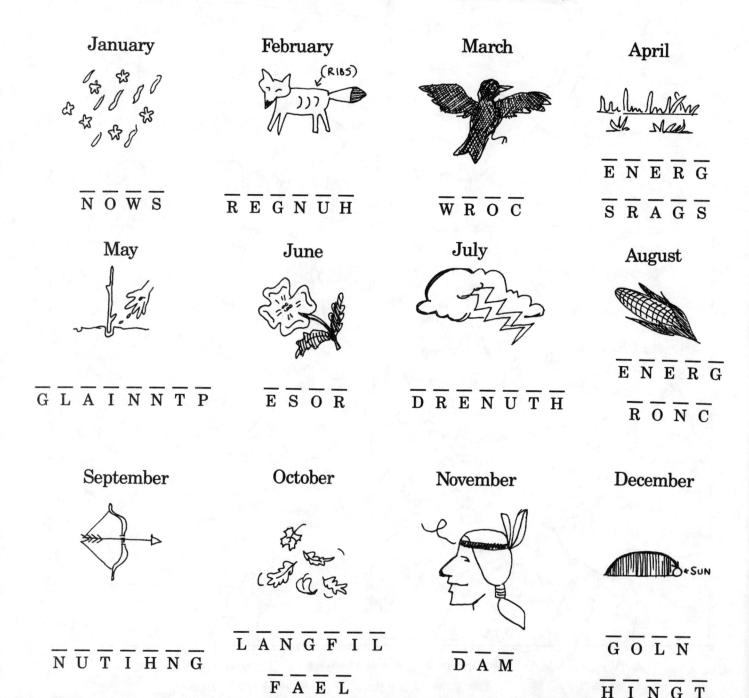

January

N O W S

February

(RIBS)

R E G N U H

March

W R O C

April

E N E R G
S R A G S

May

G L A I N N T P

June

E S O R

July

D R E N U T H

August

E N E R G
R O N C

September

N U T I H N G

October

L A N G F I L
F A E L

November

D A M

December

← SUN

G O L N
H I N G T

PHASES of the MOON

When people used moon time, a month was how long it took the moon to go from dark to full and back to dark again.

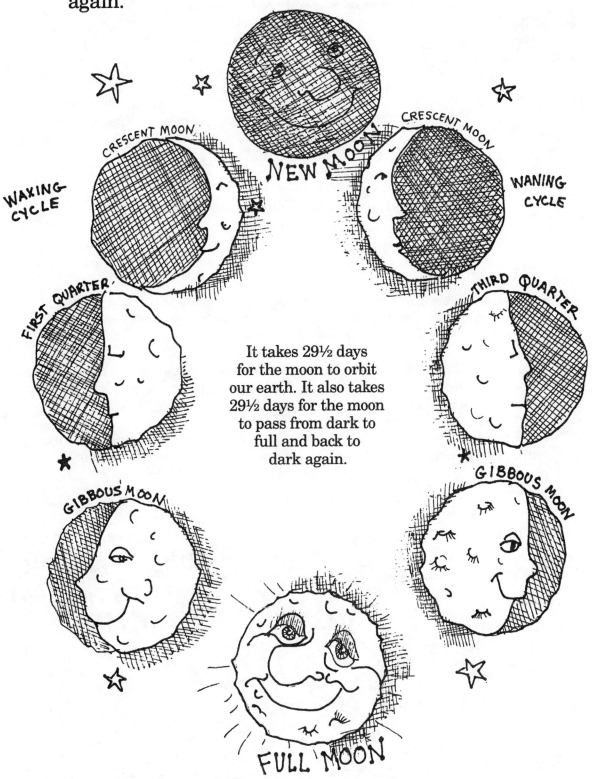

It takes 29½ days for the moon to orbit our earth. It also takes 29½ days for the moon to pass from dark to full and back to dark again.

How many different faces does the moon make each month?

MOON MATH

There are three moons, or months, in each season. How many months are there in a year?

If you had 12 months and each month had 29½ days, you would come close to making exactly one year.

But not quite!

If you multiply 12 x 29½ or 29.5, what do you get?

People who kept time by the moons had trouble keeping time year after year. That's because "moon" time and "sun" time don't exactly match. "Moon" years were 11 days shorter than our "sun" years really are.

It takes the earth 365 days and a few hours to move once around the sun. Moon calendars had a year with only 354 days. What do you think happened after a few years of using moon calendars?

After many years, the day people had chosen for spring planting came in winter. If you plant a seed when the ground is too wet and cold, will it grow?

SPRING PLANTING
IS THIS THE MONTH OF MAY?

CORRECTING TIME

TIME

People need a way to tell time correctly year after year after year. One way to make "moon" time and "sun" time exactly the same is to add an extra day to some months. That's why our months are different lengths. But each month has a full moon and "no" moon.

EVERYONE MEMORIZES THIS POEM! YOU TRY IT!

Thirty days hath September,

April, June, and November;

All the rest have thirty-one,

Excepting February alone,

And that has twenty-eight days clear

And twenty-nine in each leap year.

Can you write the names of the months that have 31 days?

_____

_____

_____

About 2000 years ago, people added one extra day every four years. That's why we have Leap Year. In Leap Year, February gets this extra day, so our calendars will be correct year after year after year.

Did you know?
Over 4000 years ago, the early Egyptians found a way to count the days correctly. After watching the sun and the stars, they invented a calendar with 365 days. But because it takes exactly 365 days AND six hours for the earth to orbit the sun, even these calendars eventually became incorrect. It took about 100 years, or a century, for Egyptian calendars to get out of step with the sun.

TIME IS CONTINUOUS...

That means we can't make it start or stop.

But we can measure time. You already know that years, seasons, months, and days are ways to measure time. When you put those measurements together, you can make a calendar.

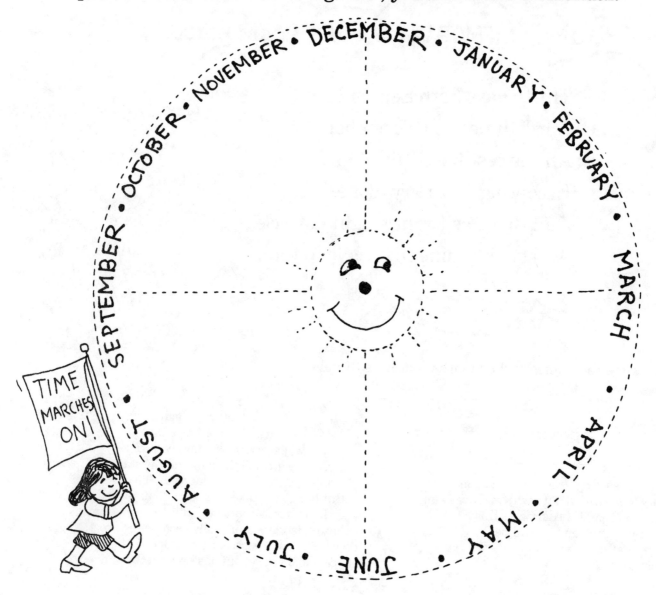

A circle calendar is fun because it shows you the different parts of a year at one time. Also, you can see that a new year picks up exactly where the old year left off.

Do you know which months make up winter? Color them blue.
Which three months come in spring? Color them yellow.
What are the months of summer? Color them green.
Which months are left? Those must be fall. Color them red.

DAYS OF THE WEEK

SUN'S DAY

PANCAKE TUESDAY

BLUE MONDAY

"RAIN ON MONDAY, SUNSHINE NEXT SUNDAY."

SATURDAY NIGHT BATH

MAUNDY THURSDAY

MOON'S DAY

"THURSDAY WE KISS, FRIDAY WE CRY, SATURDAY'S HOURS SEEM ALMOST TO FLY!"

There were years, months, even days on the calendar before humans "invented" weeks. In the Middle East and Africa, market was held several times a month. Weeks became a way to measure the time between market days. In Africa, weeks used to be four days long. The Romans, who ruled the countries around the Mediterranean Sea, had weeks of eight days.

Some people thought seven was a magic number. It takes the moon seven days to pass from one phase to another. Buddhists, Christians, and Jews believe God made the earth in seven days. For these reasons, our week now has seven days.

Each day in the week had a special meaning to early people. They named the days after the sun, moon, and stars—and the gods they thought lived there. Saturday was named for Saturn. How do you think Sunday and Monday got their names?

For years, people did different jobs on different days of the week. Do you know this old rhyme?

Wash on Monday

Iron on Tuesday

Bake on Wednesday

 Brew on Thursday

Churn on Friday

Mend on Saturday

Go to meeting on Sunday

Would you like to rename a day of the week? What name would you give it?

T.G.I.F.

Even now, each weekday may have a different meaning. Which is your favorite day of the week? Why?

What day of the week is your birthday this year? Look at a calendar to find out.

Does each year begin with the same day of the week?

MAKE YOUR OWN CALENDAR

The next pages are for you to cut out and use. Start with whatever month it is now. (Most calendars begin with the new year in January, but this one works for any month, any year. You will need to check with a current calendar to get the dates to match the days of the week. Ask a grown-up to share a regular calendar with you.)

Cut out the pages along the dotted lines. Carefully cut out the holes, or use a hole punch. You might want to put reinforcement rings on both sides of the holes. Then run a piece of string or yarn through each hole.

Once your calendar is put together, turn to whatever month it is now. Write the month in the little box, then draw your own picture of the month in the big space. You can cut out a picture from a magazine, if you'd rather. Or make a collage of things that remind you of this month (leaves and pressed flowers or snapshots are fun to use.) Next, write the correct dates in the little boxes under the days of the week, by checking another calendar. What day of the week begins this month?

Check the Table of Contents for holidays and special events each month. Look for our little calendars on the month pages for important dates. Then find the activities and enjoy! Ask your family for special days, too. (You can draw a cake for a birthday, hearts for an anniversary, a tooth for a visit to the dentist, and a baseball for Little League games.) Don't forget to mark Scouts, days without school, or your favorite TV shows.

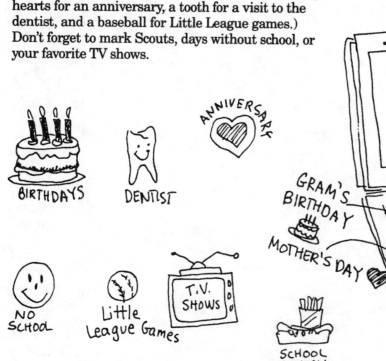

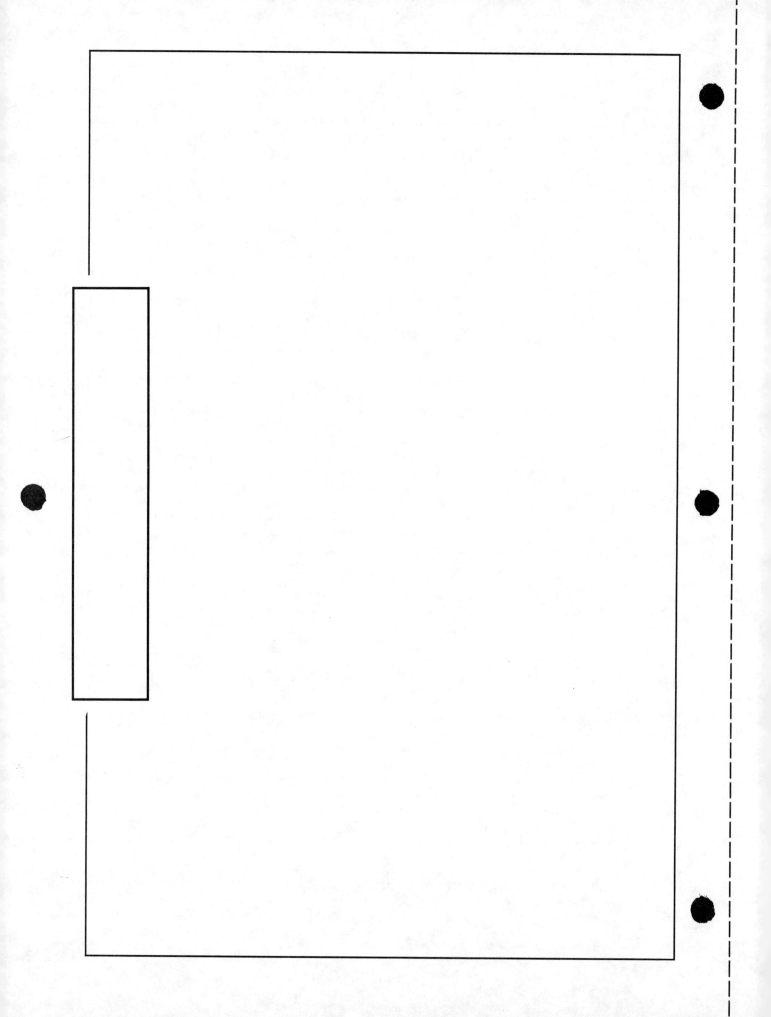

SUNDAY	MONDAY	TUESDAY	WEDNESDAY	THURSDAY	FRIDAY	SATURDAY

SUNDAY	MONDAY	TUESDAY	WEDNESDAY	THURSDAY	FRIDAY	SATURDAY

SUNDAY	MONDAY	TUESDAY	WEDNESDAY	THURSDAY	FRIDAY	SATURDAY

SUNDAY	MONDAY	TUESDAY	WEDNESDAY	THURSDAY	FRIDAY	SATURDAY

SUNDAY	MONDAY	TUESDAY	WEDNESDAY	THURSDAY	FRIDAY	SATURDAY

SUNDAY	MONDAY	TUESDAY	WEDNESDAY	THURSDAY	FRIDAY	SATURDAY

SUNDAY	MONDAY	TUESDAY	WEDNESDAY	THURSDAY	FRIDAY	SATURDAY

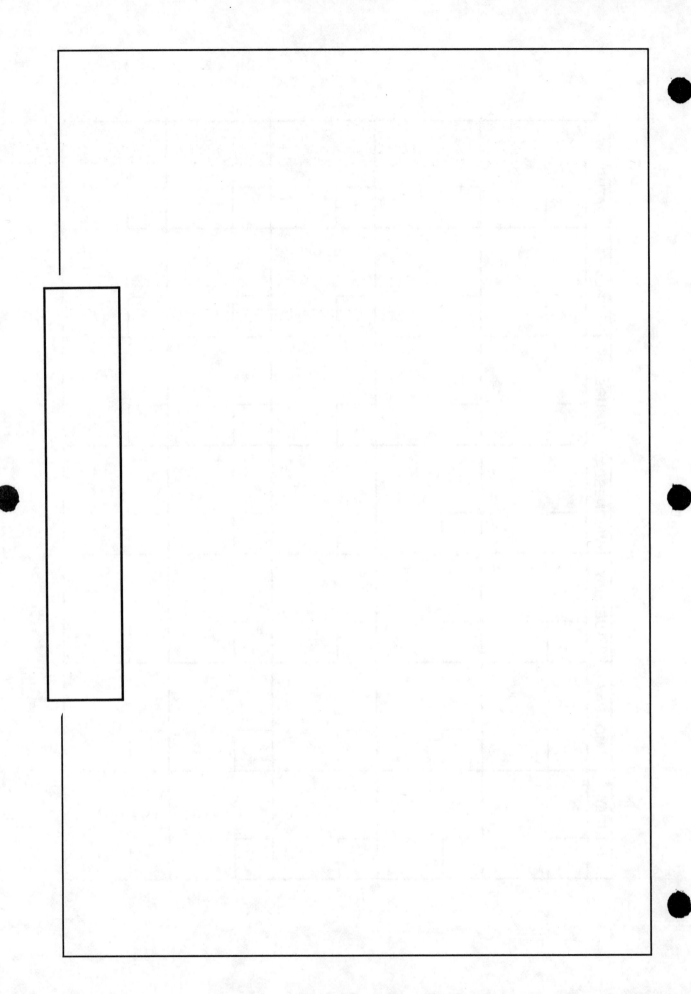

SUNDAY	MONDAY	TUESDAY	WEDNESDAY	THURSDAY	FRIDAY	SATURDAY

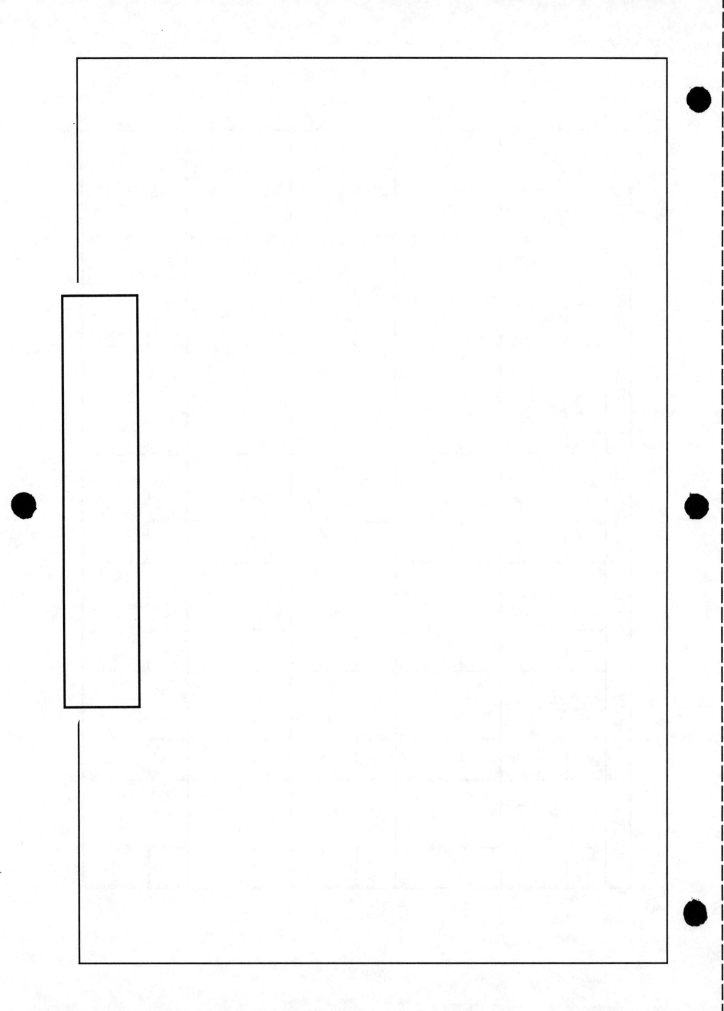

SUNDAY	MONDAY	TUESDAY	WEDNESDAY	THURSDAY	FRIDAY	SATURDAY

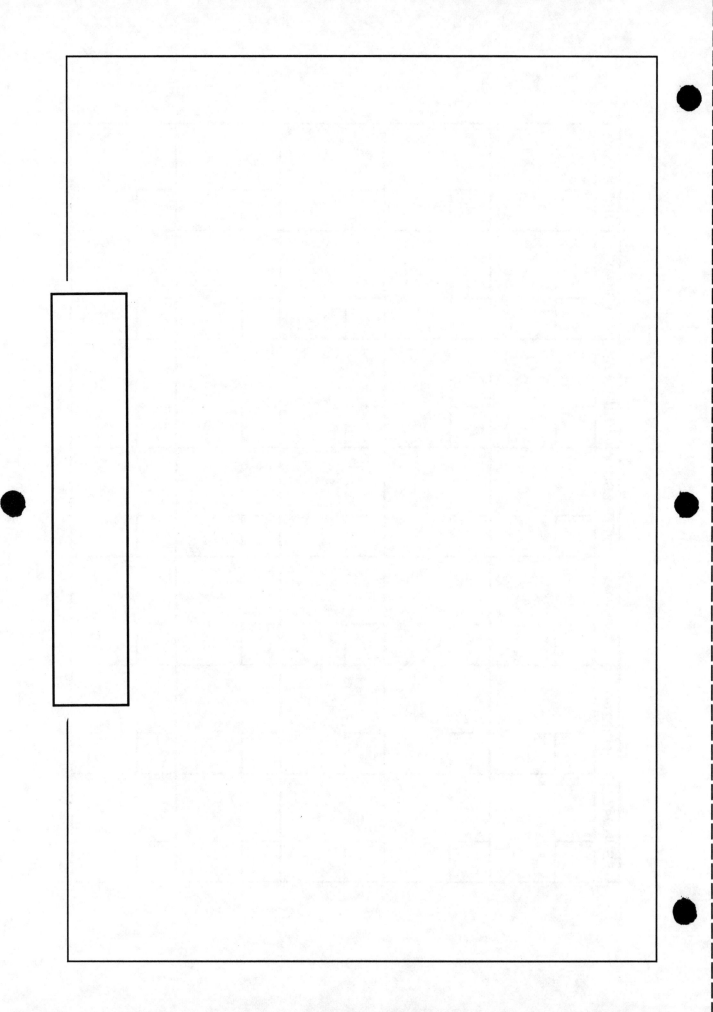

SUNDAY	MONDAY	TUESDAY	WEDNESDAY	THURSDAY	FRIDAY	SATURDAY

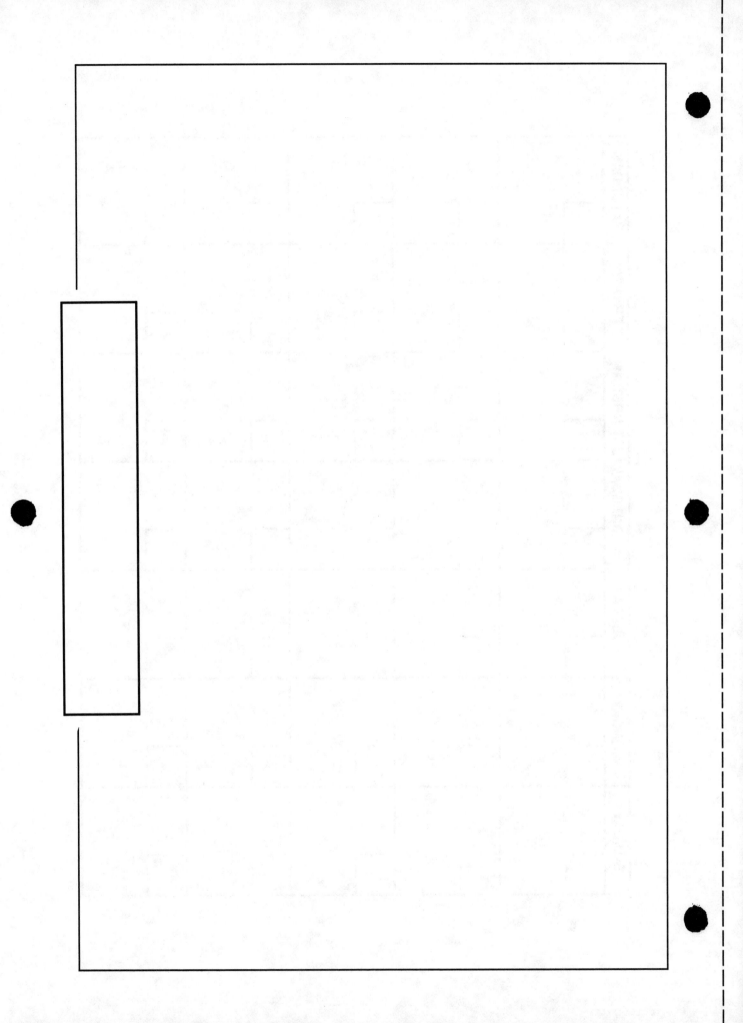

SUNDAY	MONDAY	TUESDAY	WEDNESDAY	THURSDAY	FRIDAY	SATURDAY

SUNDAY	MONDAY	TUESDAY	WEDNESDAY	THURSDAY	FRIDAY	SATURDAY

ACTIVITIES

PLEASE COLOR THIS PAGE!

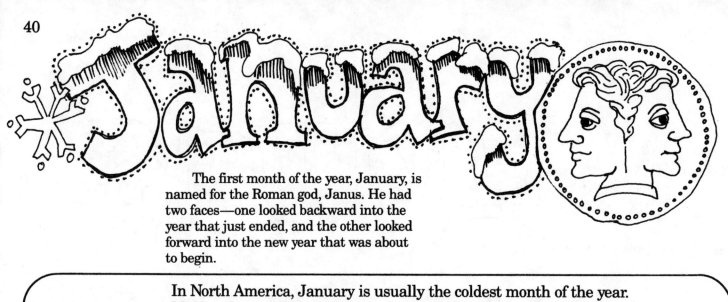

January

The first month of the year, January, is named for the Roman god, Janus. He had two faces—one looked backward into the year that just ended, and the other looked forward into the new year that was about to begin.

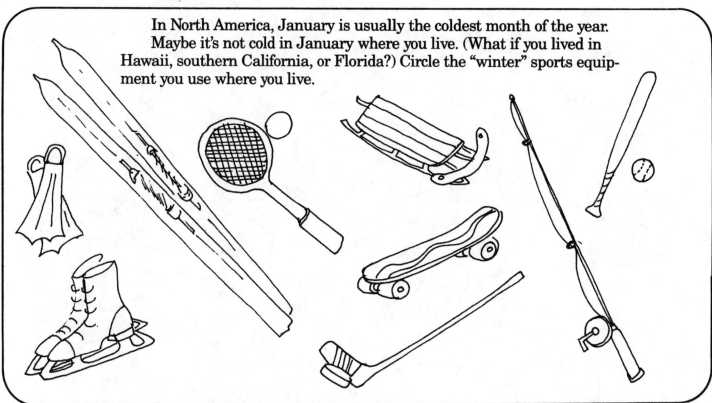

In North America, January is usually the coldest month of the year. Maybe it's not cold in January where you live. (What if you lived in Hawaii, southern California, or Florida?) Circle the "winter" sports equipment you use where you live.

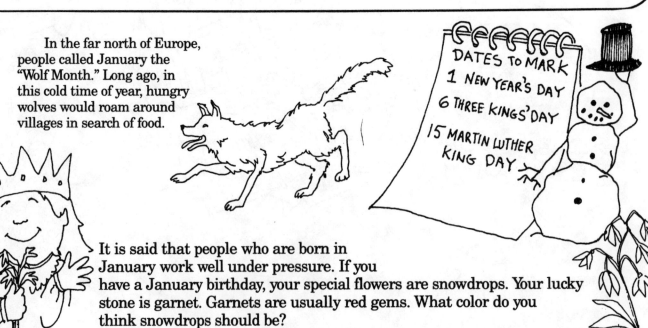

In the far north of Europe, people called January the "Wolf Month." Long ago, in this cold time of year, hungry wolves would roam around villages in search of food.

DATES TO MARK
1 NEW YEAR'S DAY
6 THREE KINGS' DAY
15 MARTIN LUTHER KING DAY

It is said that people who are born in January work well under pressure. If you have a January birthday, your special flowers are snowdrops. Your lucky stone is garnet. Garnets are usually red gems. What color do you think snowdrops should be?

January Average Temperature

Do you have a thermometer outdoors? Can you add and divide? If so, find the average temperature where you live for the coldest month of the year, January.

Write down the temperature on your calendar every day for the whole month. Try to check the thermometer at the same time each day.

At the end of the month, add up all the temperatures and divide by the number of days in the month. (Do you remember how many days there are in January?) That will give you the average temperature for that time of day during this month.

*"January brings the snow,
Makes our feet and fingers glow"*

How to Make Paper Snowflakes

You need:

- Pieces of white paper (They can be different sizes)
- Scissors
- Transparent tape
- Thread

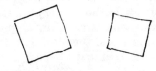

1. Cut the paper into squares.

2. Make a triangle by folding one corner to the opposite corner.

3. Fold one of the two long points so it overlaps the opposite side.

4. Fold the other long point across the other side.

5. Fold the entire piece of paper down the middle.

6. Cut designs along all the edges.

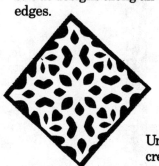

Unfold the paper to see your creation.

You can make a paper snowstorm in your windows.

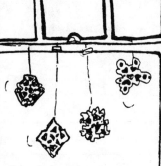

Cut thread into various lengths.

Tape one end of each thread to the snowflake.

Tape the other end to a window frame.

DID YOU FOLD 4 TIMES?

HAPPY NEW YEAR

We celebrate the end of the old year and the beginning of the new one on New Year's Eve. On this last night of the year, people wear funny hats, make lots of noise, and throw confetti, especially at the stroke of midnight. A whole new year begins then.

New Year's Day, January 1, is the time to give up bad habits and start some good ones. New Year's resolutions are promises you make to yourself—and try to keep for the whole year. You might promise to brush your teeth twice a day or do your homework on time. Can you think of some other resolutions? If you keep them, maybe you'll be allowed to stay up late next New Year's Eve. And make noise at midnight.

CUSTOMS AROUND THE WORLD

CLEAN SLATE

START OFF ON THE 'RIGHT FOOT'

In Japan, New Year's Day is the biggest celebration of the year. It is called *O-shogatsu*. Long ago everyone in Japan became a year older on this day. Imagine everybody in the country having a birthday party at the same time! Many Japanese send New Year's cards—and the mailman delivers them all on the same day!

On the Japanese New Year's Eve, at the stroke of midnight everybody starts to laugh. This is said to bring good luck. The next morning they take a bath, put on clean clothing, and are fresh for the new year.

Not everybody celebrates the new year on January 1st. In India, the new year starts with a festival in December. The Chinese New Year comes in late January or early February and lasts for two weeks. For people of the Jewish faith the new year begins in September or October. It is called Rosh Hashanah.

NEW YEAR'S DAY

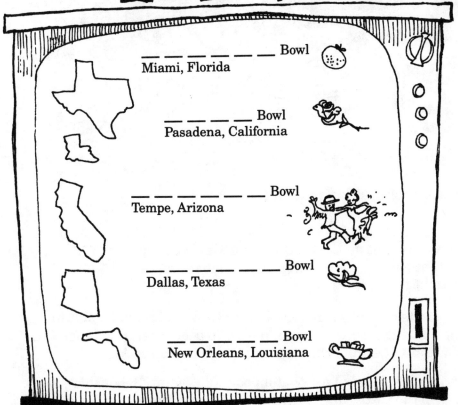

_ _ _ _ _ _ Bowl
Miami, Florida

_ _ _ _ _ Bowl
Pasadena, California

_ _ _ _ _ _ _ Bowl
Tempe, Arizona

_ _ _ _ _ Bowl
Dallas, Texas

_ _ _ _ _ Bowl
New Orleans, Louisiana

On New Year's Day many people sleep late because they were partying late the night before. No sooner are the sleepyheads up and about than they sit down in front of the TV to watch college football games. These are called "bowl" games. Do you know why? They are played in stadiums that are shaped like bowls.

Some of the bowl games played on New Year's Day are shown on the TV screen to the left. Unscramble their names and fill in the blanks. Then draw a line from the symbol to the state where it is played.

GEAONR   ISTFEA

SERO

RGAUS   TNOOTC

Who Won The Game?

The New York Knee Knockers and the California Crushers had a close game. Can you add up the points and name the winner?

The Knee Knockers scored 3 touchdowns, 2 extra points, 3 field goals, and 1 safety.

The Crushers scored 2 touchdowns, 2 extra points, 4 field goals, and 2 safeties.

SCORING POINTS

Touchdown = 6 Points

Extra point = 1 Point

Field goal = 3 Points

Safety = 2 Points

Knee Knockers ☐ ☐
☐ ☐

Crushers

Point spread _____

Put the final score on the scoreboard.

THREE KINGS' DAY JAN. 6th

January 6th is part of Christmas that lasts into the New Year! This is Three Kings' Day.

In countries as different as Egypt, Italy, and Mexico, people remember the star that led three wise kings to find a baby in a stable. And the gifts they brought him.

In Mexico, parts of South America, Puerto Rico, and Spain, children leave straw for the kings' camels before they go to bed. When they wake up the next morning, they find their shoes filled with candies!

Russian children believe that a poor old woman, Baboushka, was too busy to help the three kings find Jesus. Because she was sorry she didn't help, she still brings presents to boys and girls.

In Italy, the good fairy Befana is a little like Baboushka. She brings gifts to all good children.

In France, children celebrate Three Kings' Day by eating cake. The youngest gets to serve everyone else. And children wear crowns, just like the kings did so long ago.

Make a King's Crown!

Do you know how to make a crown?
You need:
- One piece of construction paper (9 × 12)
- Pencil
- Scissors
- Transparent tape
- Pieces of shiny paper (scraps from candy, foil, left-over Christmas wrappings work well)
- White glue

4. Overlap one end and tape.
5. Wrap the crown around your head, and tape to fit.

1. Fold paper in half.
2. Draw crown points along the folded edge.
3. Cut along pencil lines.

6. Decorate with shiny paper jewels.

Holiday Cake Recipe

Would you like to bake a cake for Three Kings' Day? Here is an easy recipe you can use for all sorts of holidays and special occasions throughout the year. Ask a grown-up to help you get started. Or if you are already a good cook, you might try tripling this recipe for a three-layer THREE KINGS' CAKE!

"I Made It Myself" Cake

You will need:
9-inch cake pan (round or square) and margarine or vegetable oil to
   grease it
1 cup flour
1 cup sugar
1 teaspoon baking powder
1 cup water **or** orange juice
1 egg
1 teaspoonful vanilla **or** grated orange peel
1/3 cup vegetable oil

- Turn on the oven to 350 degrees.
- Oil or grease the cake pan.

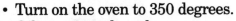

- Sift flour, sugar, and baking powder together in a big bowl. Mix well.

- Add the rest of the ingredients. Beat together until the batter is smooth.

- Pour batter into the cake pan.

- Put cake in the oven and bake about 35 minutes. (To see if your cake is done, stick a toothpick in the middle. If it comes out clean, the cake is cooked all the way through!)

- Let the cake cool, then cover it with a flat plate.
- Turn the cake over and ice if you want.
(Strawberry preserves make an easy icing for a one-layer cake! And a traditional one for Three Kings' Day.)

To make a Valentine Cake:
Double recipe.
Add 2/3 cup cocoa
and 1/4 cup red coloring.

To make a Birthday Cake:
Stir "favors" into batter
(wrap coins, a ring, a whistle, or
a thimble in foil.)

Use two pans:
one round, and one square.
Cut round cake in half.

Bake in a round moon shaped pan.
Frost with your favorite icing,
and decorate with candles.

Martin Luther King's Birthday

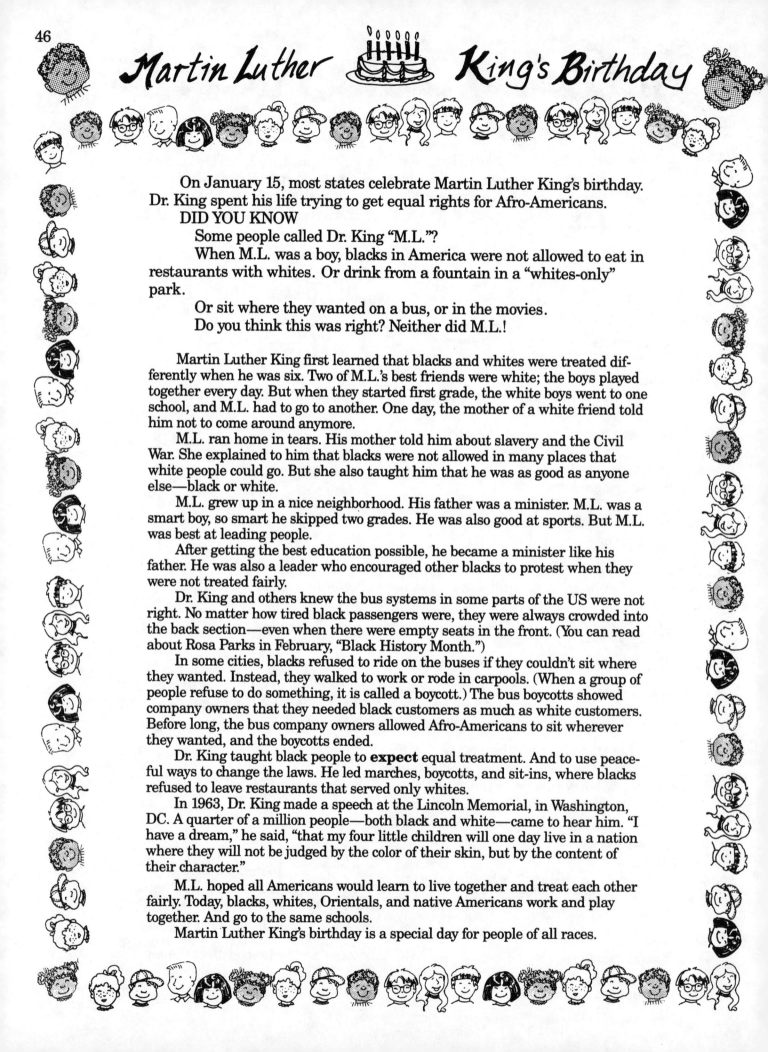

On January 15, most states celebrate Martin Luther King's birthday. Dr. King spent his life trying to get equal rights for Afro-Americans.

DID YOU KNOW

Some people called Dr. King "M.L."?

When M.L. was a boy, blacks in America were not allowed to eat in restaurants with whites. Or drink from a fountain in a "whites-only" park.

Or sit where they wanted on a bus, or in the movies.

Do you think this was right? Neither did M.L.!

Martin Luther King first learned that blacks and whites were treated differently when he was six. Two of M.L.'s best friends were white; the boys played together every day. But when they started first grade, the white boys went to one school, and M.L. had to go to another. One day, the mother of a white friend told him not to come around anymore.

M.L. ran home in tears. His mother told him about slavery and the Civil War. She explained to him that blacks were not allowed in many places that white people could go. But she also taught him that he was as good as anyone else—black or white.

M.L. grew up in a nice neighborhood. His father was a minister. M.L. was a smart boy, so smart he skipped two grades. He was also good at sports. But M.L. was best at leading people.

After getting the best education possible, he became a minister like his father. He was also a leader who encouraged other blacks to protest when they were not treated fairly.

Dr. King and others knew the bus systems in some parts of the US were not right. No matter how tired black passengers were, they were always crowded into the back section—even when there were empty seats in the front. (You can read about Rosa Parks in February, "Black History Month.")

In some cities, blacks refused to ride on the buses if they couldn't sit where they wanted. Instead, they walked to work or rode in carpools. (When a group of people refuse to do something, it is called a boycott.) The bus boycotts showed company owners that they needed black customers as much as white customers. Before long, the bus company owners allowed Afro-Americans to sit wherever they wanted, and the boycotts ended.

Dr. King taught black people to **expect** equal treatment. And to use peaceful ways to change the laws. He led marches, boycotts, and sit-ins, where blacks refused to leave restaurants that served only whites.

In 1963, Dr. King made a speech at the Lincoln Memorial, in Washington, DC. A quarter of a million people—both black and white—came to hear him. "I have a dream," he said, "that my four little children will one day live in a nation where they will not be judged by the color of their skin, but by the content of their character."

M.L. hoped all Americans would learn to live together and treat each other fairly. Today, blacks, whites, Orientals, and native Americans work and play together. And go to the same schools.

Martin Luther King's birthday is a special day for people of all races.

Help Celebrate M.L.'s Birthday by coloring this page!

CHINESE NEW YEAR

Did you know that people of Chinese descent celebrate the new year for 15 days?

The Chinese celebrate with the Festival of Lanterns. They hold parades with thousands of lanterns lighting the way for the new year. You might want to go to Chinatown in a city like New York or San Francisco during this festival. You can see the new year marching in the streets. One year will be a dragon; another a pig. You may hear firecrackers. And if you are very lucky, you will get to smell and taste some wonderful Chinese food!

APREP   SODNOLE   KCOLC   LACROUCTAL   KOCTER

Can you name these Chinese inventions?

Did You Know?

On New Year's Day, Chinese-American children wake up to find something very special under their pillows — a red envelope with money in it. (Red means good luck to the Chinese.)

MAKE A DRAGON FINGER PUPPET

You need:

- 2 raisin or Jello boxes
- Transparent tape
- Colored construction paper, including red
- ½-inch styrofoam balls (cut in half) for eyes

1. Cover boxes with colored paper, leaving one end open for your fingers.
2. Tape box lids together to make a mouth hinge.
3. Line hinged boxes with red paper to reinforce hinge, as well as create dragon's mouth.
4. Cut fringe on a strip of colored paper to decorate dragon.
5. Decorate and glue on eyes.
6. Put hand in a knee sock, putting fingers in boxes to work dragon's mouth.

49

The Chinese name each year for an animal! What kind of animal is this year?

ATR

XO ___

GTERI ___

BTIBAR ___

RNGOAD ___

ESAKN ___

REHSO ___

EPHES ___

KYONME ___

RSOTROE ___

OGD ___

IGP ___

1990 is the year of the horse. 1991 is the year of the sheep. 1992 is the year of the monkey. What animal is 1993? What year is the rabbit? When does the horse come back?

(Hint: When the year of the pig ends, the year of the rat begins.)

February

February is the shortest month of the year—usually only 28 days long. (That's good, because most people are tired of winter and want it to be over!)

If you were born in February, your lucky flowers are primroses or violets. Your gemstone is amethyst (say *AM-eh-thist*). Do you know what color it is? People with February birthdays are thought to be sincere.

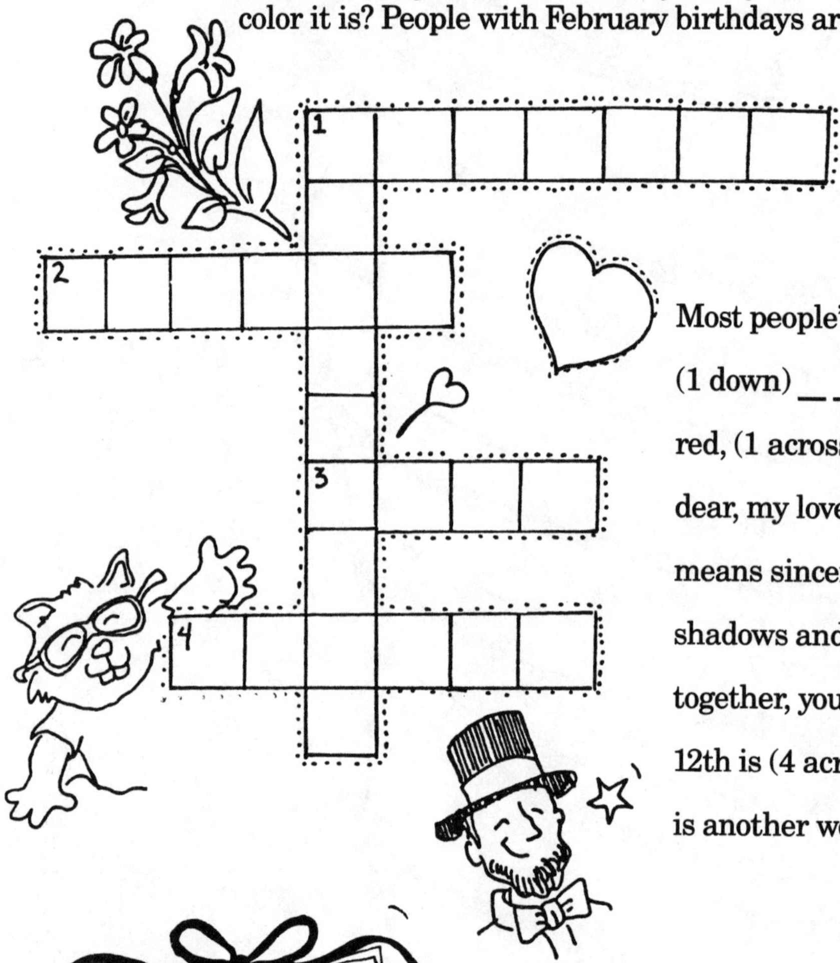

Most people's favorite holiday this month is Saint (1 down) _ _ _ _ _ _ _ _ _ _ _ 's Day. "Roses are red, (1 across) _ _ _ _ _ _ _ _ _ are blue. Believe me, dear, my love is (3 across) _ _ _ _ _ ." (hint: this word means sincere). February's birthstone is the color of shadows and sunsets. If you mix pink and light blue together, you make (2 across) _ _ _ _ _ _ _ _. The 12th is (4 across) _ _ _ _ _ _ _ Abe's birthday. (This is another word for sincere.)

CALENDAR DATES

12 Lincoln's Birthday
14 Valentine's Day
22 Washington's Birthday

(Third Monday in month is Presidents' Day— Federal Holiday)

BEWARE THIN ICE

"February brings the rain, Thaws the frozen lake again."

Leap Year

Did you read about time in the beginning of this book? Then you know Leap Year is one way we keep our calendars from getting out of step with the sun's time. Every four years, February gets an extra day. When it has 29 days, it's called Leap Year.

Most people don't want to be born on February 29. Do you know why? Well, let's pretend you were born on February 29, 1984. How many birthdays would you have had? (Don't forget, February 29 comes only once ever four years.) How old would you really be?

1984 and 1988 were leap years. When will the next leap year come?

This month starts with the letter "__".

MR. FROG'S MOUTH IS FULL OF THINGS THAT START WITH "F."

HOW MANY can you Name?

February is Black History Month

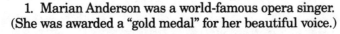

1. Marian Anderson was a world-famous opera singer. (She was awarded a "gold medal" for her beautiful voice.)

2. Arthur Ashe was not only a famous tennis player. He also wrote a book for anyone who wants to learn to play tennis well, *Getting Started in Tennis*.

3. George Washington Carver was an important educator, farmer and scientist. (He found lots of good ways to use the peanut, sweet potato, and soybean.)

4. A black man, Matthew Henson, was among the first people to reach the North Pole—along with Admiral Peary and 4 Eskimos.

5. Barbara Jordan was the first black in this century to become a state senator. She also served as a diplomat to China and even had her picture on the cover of TIME Magazine.

6. Thurgood Marshall was the first Afro-American to serve on the Supreme Court. He was one of the top judges in our country.

7. Rosa Parks made her living by sewing. Once, when she was tired from a long day at work, a bus driver asked her to give up her seat to a white man. Rosa refused and went to jail. A boycott of the bus company began. Because Rosa and others stood up for their rights, blacks were finally allowed to sit wherever they wanted on a bus.

8. Harriet Tubman was a Maryland slave who ran away to freedom. People called her "Moses" because she risked her life again and again to lead other slaves to Canada. When the Civil War broke out, she became a valuable scout for Union troops.

9. Almost 100 years ago, a black doctor, named Daniel Hale Williams, performed the first successful operation EVER on a human heart!

10. Did you know the Harlem Globetrotters had a woman player? Lynette Woodward broke all sorts of women's basketball records, and even won an Olympic Gold Medal. But her proudest moment came when she was selected to join the Globetrotters.

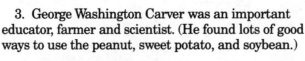
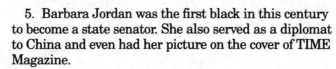
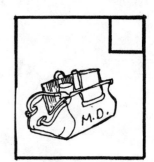
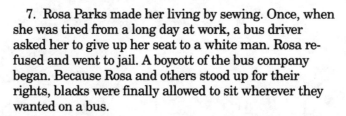

After reading about these famous Afro-Americans, see if you can put the correct number in the little box inside each picture.

Ground Hog Day

Ground Hog Day is February 2nd.

Do you know the superstition about this day? If a ground hog comes out of his burrow and sees his shadow, it is said that he will go back inside and sleep for six more weeks. This means six more weeks of winter. People who are ready for spring hope February 2nd is cloudy.

MAKE MR. GROUND HOG

You need:

- 1 blue sheet of 9" x 12" construction paper
- 1 brown sheet of 9" x 12" construction paper
- White chalk or crayon
- Popsicle stick
- Tape and scissors

1. Draw Mr. Ground Hog on brown paper. Draw him as wide as your hand.

2. Cut out Mr. Ground Hog. Tape him to a popsicle stick.

3. To make hole in ground:

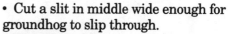

- Cut a slit in middle wide enough for groundhog to slip through.
- Draw lines from ends of the slit to the edges of paper.
- Color the ground (below the slit) white to look like snow.
- Add flakes to sky or draw a big sun.

SHADOW PLAY

Place your hands between a light and the wall.
Move hands slightly and make the sounds animals make.

GOOSE

BIRD

RABBIT

SNAKE

VALENTINE'S DAY is ALWAYS CELEBRATED ON FEB. 14

February 14 is Valentine's Day. Like many special days, Valentine customs come from many different lands.

Long, long ago, the Romans held a festival for the god Saturn. They thought he protected them from hungry wolves. At Saturn's festival, young people drew each others' names out of a bowl. They would be partners for dances. Sometimes, they became sweethearts.

Later, there was a Christian priest named Valentine. He loved children and always gave them flowers from his garden. The Roman emperor put Valentine in prison because he would not worship the many Roman gods. But the children remembered their friend. They sent "love notes" to Valentine in jail.

In England, when the birds began to build their nests, people would think about love and marriage. Children went from house to house chanting verses, and often people tossed flowers or pennies to them.

German girls attached names of boys they liked to onions. On Valentine's Day, they would plant the onions in pots. The first one to sprout was said to be the boy the girl would marry.

In France people held fancy-dress balls on Valentine's Day. A man might give his sweetheart a heart-shaped box with a verse he had written. Others gave ladies lockets or whatever they could afford.

Some Valentines use a puzzle, known as a rebus.

A rebus uses a picture in place of letters or words.

Can you read the rebus messages below?

Write the correct words next to the picture puzzle.

You don't have to be in love with someone to give him or her a Valentine!

HAPPY VALENTINE'S DAY

What Doesn't Belong on Valentine's Day? (Draw a heart around the pictures that remind you of this holiday. Cross out the pictures that go with other holidays.)

♡ EVERYONE CAN "HAVE A HEART"!

To make your own Valentine, you need:

- red construction paper
- a pencil
- scissors

1. Fold a piece of construction paper in half.

2. Draw the shape of an ear.

(Pretend the fold is where the ear joins the head.)

3. Keep the paper folded, as you cut out the heart.

 4. Keep practicing!

A VALENTINE FOR A HEART-BREAKER!

Write a message and decorate a heart you have cut out.

Cut the heart into several pieces.

Put the pieces in an envelope and give it to a friend.

How many ways can you say "I LOVE YOU?"
In French, it's Je t'aime (say ZHE TEM).
In Italian, it's Io ti amo (say EEYO TEE AHMO).
In Russian, it's Я ТЕБЯ ЛЮБЛЮ (say YA TEBYA LOOBLUE).
In Swedish, it's Jag älskar dig (say YOG ELSKAR DAY).

Two important presidents of the United States were born this month: Abraham Lincoln on February 12 and George Washington on February 22.

We celebrate both birthdays on the third Monday of the month. This holiday is called Presidents' Day.

You see pictures of these presidents every day. George Washington's face is on a quarter. Abraham Lincoln's is on a penny. Place the face side of a quarter under this page. Line it up under the large circle and rub with a pencil. George Washington's face will appear above his name. For Abraham Lincoln, place a penny under the smaller circle and do the same.

George Washington

Abraham Lincoln

This president learned to write with a buzzard's feather. He also read a book every chance he got—sometimes by the light of a fire, at other times while he was plowing the fields.

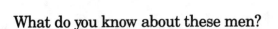

What do you know about these men?

Draw a line from your rubbing of each president's face to the stories about him.

This president grew up on a farm, called a plantation, in Virginia. He learned to ride a pony as soon as his legs were long enough to reach the stirrups.

This president first learned about slavery on a flatboat trip down the Mississippi River to New Orleans. He thought it was wrong for one man to own another. When he became president, he freed the slaves.

This president was called the "Father of his Country," even though he had no children of his own. He was a good stepfather to his wife's children.

His nickname was "Honest _ _ _." Once by mistake, he charged a woman too much for things she bought in his store. He walked for three miles to give her back the money he owed her.

George Washington slept here

‒ ‒ ‒ ‒ ‒ ‒ ‒ ‒ ‒ ‒ ‒
N U M T O   N N R V E O

PRESIDENTS' RESIDENCES

ABE LINCOLN'S LOG CABIN

You need:

- School size milk (or cream) carton
- Corrugated lightbulb package (4 bulb size)
- Glue
- Scissors
- Brown marker
- Construction paper

1. Unfold the lightbulb box and turn it inside out.

2. Turn the milk container on its side and trace its outline on the lightbulb box. (Make sure the ridges of the box are sideways, like logs. Trace the sides with the peaks twice, and the front and back once.)

3. Cut out the four sections.

4. Color them with your marker.

5. Glue the cut-outs to the milk carton.

6. Add folded construction paper for the roof and chimney.

ONE STEP FURTHER:
Make a diorama with a shoe box cover. Add gravel, grass, and twigs for trees and fences.

MARDI GRAS

Mardi Gras is French for "Fat Tuesday," when people fill up on their favorite foods before fasting for Lent. Sometimes this day is called Pancake Tuesday.

Here is an easy pancake recipe to try:

½ cup milk　　2 tablespoons vegetable oil　　1 egg　　1 cup enriched flour　　2 teaspoons baking powder　　2 tablespoons sugar

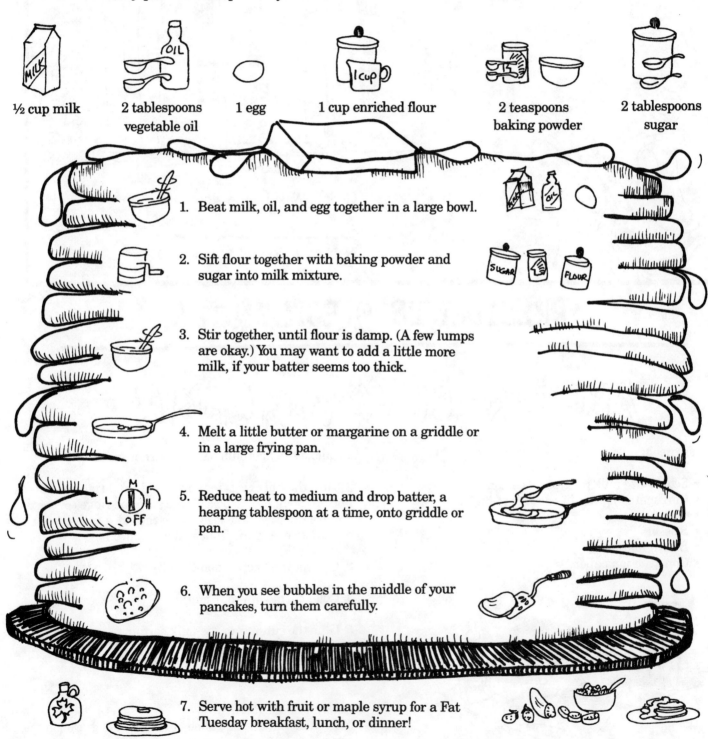

1. Beat milk, oil, and egg together in a large bowl.

2. Sift flour together with baking powder and sugar into milk mixture.

3. Stir together, until flour is damp. (A few lumps are okay.) You may want to add a little more milk, if your batter seems too thick.

4. Melt a little butter or margarine on a griddle or in a large frying pan.

5. Reduce heat to medium and drop batter, a heaping tablespoon at a time, onto griddle or pan.

6. When you see bubbles in the middle of your pancakes, turn them carefully.

7. Serve hot with fruit or maple syrup for a Fat Tuesday breakfast, lunch, or dinner!

Lent often begins in February. For forty days, Christians around the world prepare for Easter by giving up something they enjoy – like candy, soft drinks, or sleeping late.

But before Lent begins, people like to celebrate. At Carnival in South America and Mardi Gras in New Orleans, people dress up and parade through the streets. These noisy celebrations last for two or three days.

Here's how to make your own zany Mardi Gras mask:

You need:
- Brown paper bag
- Crayon
- Scissors
- Glue
- Odds and ends
  (see step 4 below)

1. Put the bag on over your head. If it is too long, take it off and cut slits on the sides, so it fits over shoulders.

2. Put the bag on again, and mark lightly with a crayon where your eyes go.

3. Take the bag off, and cut holes for your eyes.

4. Glue on anything you like: buttons, empty toilet paper rolls, colorful yarn, wrapping paper, wallpaper scraps, straws. Use your imagination and make the mask look as zany as possible.

Find the two masks that are *exactly* alike.

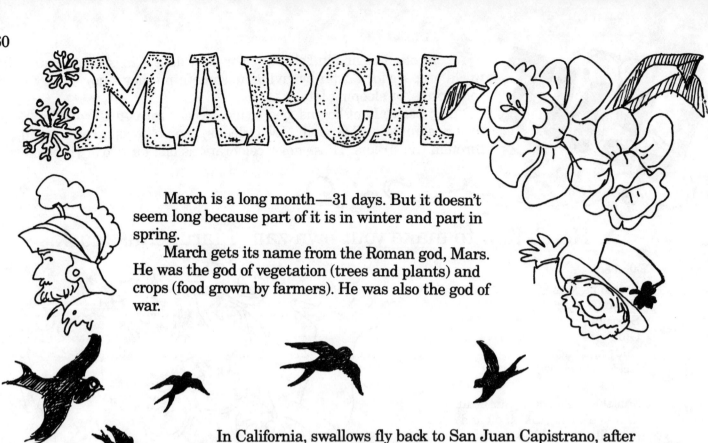

MARCH

March is a long month—31 days. But it doesn't seem long because part of it is in winter and part in spring.

March gets its name from the Roman god, Mars. He was the god of vegetation (trees and plants) and crops (food grown by farmers). He was also the god of war.

In California, swallows fly back to San Juan Capistrano, after spending the winter in South America. The first ones arrive at the same time every year, around March 19.

On March 24, the world's longest dogsled race is held in Alaska. It goes from Anchorage to Nome—a distance of more than 500 miles.

In Finland, the Lapps have reindeer races. Men and women on skis compete to see who can round up 100 reindeer the fastest.

There are lots of festivals around the world in March. In Australia the Aborigines have a "Moomba" Festival. "Moomba" means, "Let's Party!" People in Melbourne, Australia celebrate with fireworks and music. In Japan, they have a special festival of dolls.

CALENDAR DATES

3- DOLL'S DAY

17-ST. PATRICK'S DAY

21- FIRST DAY OF SPRING

How may words can you make out of the word FESTIVAL?

_____

_____

_____

_____

Can you guess what March's flower is? The daffodil. That's a pretty good sign of spring, don't you think? If you were born this month, bloodstone is your lucky gemstone.

"MARCH COMES IN LIKE A LION AND GOES OUT LIKE A LAMB"

PAPER LION

You need:

- Yellow and orange construction paper
- Pencil
- Paper plate
- Paste or glue
- Crayons

1. Cut paper into 3" x 1" strips.
2. Wrap strips around a pencil to curl.

3. Paste the curls around rim of the plate.
   (Alternate yellow and orange)

4. Draw lion's face, and color with crayons.

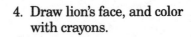

eyes nose mouth freckles

Wooly Lamb

You need:

- White index card (without lines)
- Black marker
- 8 or more cotton balls
- White glue

1. Fold index card in half (the short way).

2. Cut out a rectangle between the legs (save the piece you cut out).

3. With the piece you cut out, make head by cutting off the front corners to form a curve.

4. Cut slits at the back of the head and the front of the body.

5. Blacken end of head for snout. Blacken four legs.

6. Slip head into body.

7. Cover the body with a thin layer of glue.

8. Stretch cotton balls and attach to head and body.

9. Add little paper triangles for ears.

MARCH BREEZES LOUD AND SHRILL to stir the DANCING DAFFODIL

March is a windy month. In the northeastern part of the United States, the wind is still cold and wet. But in the Midwest, it is often warm and dry.

CHINOOK WIND

"SNOW EATER"

NORTHWEST ← MIDWEST → NORTHEAST

This wind is called the Chinook. It is named after an Indian tribe that lived along the north Pacific coast where the wind comes from. It starts out with lots of moisture from the ocean. But as it blows inland and rises over the Rocky Mountains, it becomes hot and dry. When it reaches the Midwest, it is warm enough to raise temperatures 45 degrees in 15 minutes! That's why some people call the Chinook the "snow eater."

PIE PAN WIND CHIME

You need:
- One large aluminum foil pie pan or roll tray
- Several smaller ones of different shapes and sizes
- Hammer and nail
- String

1. With the hammer and nail, punch several holes in the large pan or tray.
2. Punch one hole near the edge of each of the smaller ones.
3. Push pieces of string through each of the holes in the large pan.
4. Tie a knot so the strings won't slide through.
5. Push the other ends of the strings through the holes in the smaller pans and tie knots.
6. Punch two holes in the large pan on opposite edges.
7. Thread a piece of string through each hole and knot at each end.

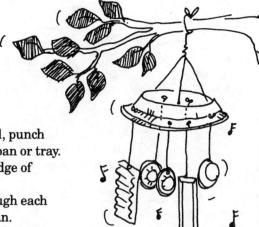

Hang in a tree and listen to the beautiful music the wind makes!

WINDY DAY ACTIVITIES

Weather vanes show which way the wind is blowing. They come in all shapes and sizes. Here is a simple one you can make:

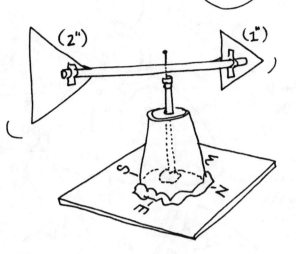

You need:
- Cardboard
- Scissors
- Transparent tape
- Plastic drinking straw
- Pencil with eraser
- Pin
- Square piece of wood
- Small paper cup
- Modeling clay

1. Cut the cardboard into two triangles—one with 2" sides, and the other with 1" sides.
2. Cut a slit in each end of the straw.

3. Slide the triangles into the slits (as shown) and hold with tape.

4. Push the pin through the middle of the straw and attach to the eraser of the pencil. (Make sure the straw can turn freely.)

5. Put clay inside the cup to hold the pencil steady.
6. Attach the cup to the board with clay.
7. Mark each side of the piece of wood with compass directions (N, E, S, and W, going clockwise).

Take your creation outside on a windy day and place the N side to the north. (The arrow of a compass always points in that direction.) The vane will point into the wind.

Put an "X" on all the things that need wind to work.

64

DoLLs' Day in Japan

March 3 is a special day in Japan. On this day children take out small dolls that their mothers gave them. Using a set of shelves, they arrange their dolls carefully—putting the emperor and empress on the top shelf. Then princes, musicians, and servants are placed below. Japanese children arrange tiny furniture and musical instruments on the bottom shelf.

COLOR THIS PAGE.

WHAT DO  YOU KNOW ABOUT THE JAPANESE?

Japan is a country made up of islands in the Pacific Ocean.

In America, people  to greet each other.

In Japan, they .

You use a when you eat.

The Japanese eat with 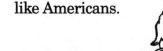 .

In most countries, we sleep in 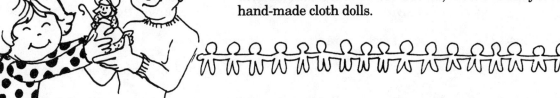 .

In Japan, people sleep on the 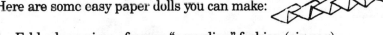 .

Still, kids in Japan like to eat  , go to  games, and watch  —just like Americans.

Like the Japanese, mothers in North America often save special dolls for their children. Sometimes, these are storybook dolls or hand-made cloth dolls.

Do you play with paper dolls? It's fun to make them, too.

Here are some easy paper dolls you can make:

1. Fold a long piece of paper "accordion" fashion (zig zag).

2. Draw a simple doll shape on the top fold. Draw arms all the way to the edges. Don't draw hands.

3. Carefully cut through all the layers. **DON'T CUT THE EDGES WHERE THE HANDS GO.**

4. Unfold. . . **LOOK AT ALL THE HAPPY DOLLS HOLDING HANDS!**

PURIM

STORY OF ESTHER

Purim is a Jewish holiday celebrated in March. It is known as the feast of lots.

Long, long ago in Persia, the king held a contest to find the most beautiful woman to be his queen. He chose Esther, a Jewish girl.

Esther was as smart as she was pretty. And she needed to be clever, because the king had a wicked adviser, Haman, who hated the Jews. The Jewish people, who believed in one God, would not bow down before this evil prince Haman.

This made Haman so angry that he decided to kill all the Jews. He convinced the king to draw a lot, called a *pur,* to decide the day the Jewish people would die.

When Esther heard of this decision, she knew she had to do something fast. She prayed that God would help her people. And she used the clever mind God had given her.

It was against the law for anyone, even the queen, to appear before the king without his invitation. So Esther decided to invite the king to a feast. He loved feasts more than almost anything.

At Esther's feast, she reminded her husband that a Jewish man, named Mordechai, had once saved his life. She pleaded with the king to save her people. He did — and hanged the wicked Haman on the very gallows he had built for the Jews.

There is a book in the Bible named for the beautiful, wise queen Esther. And in March people celebrate her bravery by reading about her and stomping every time Haman's name is read.

Purim Lots

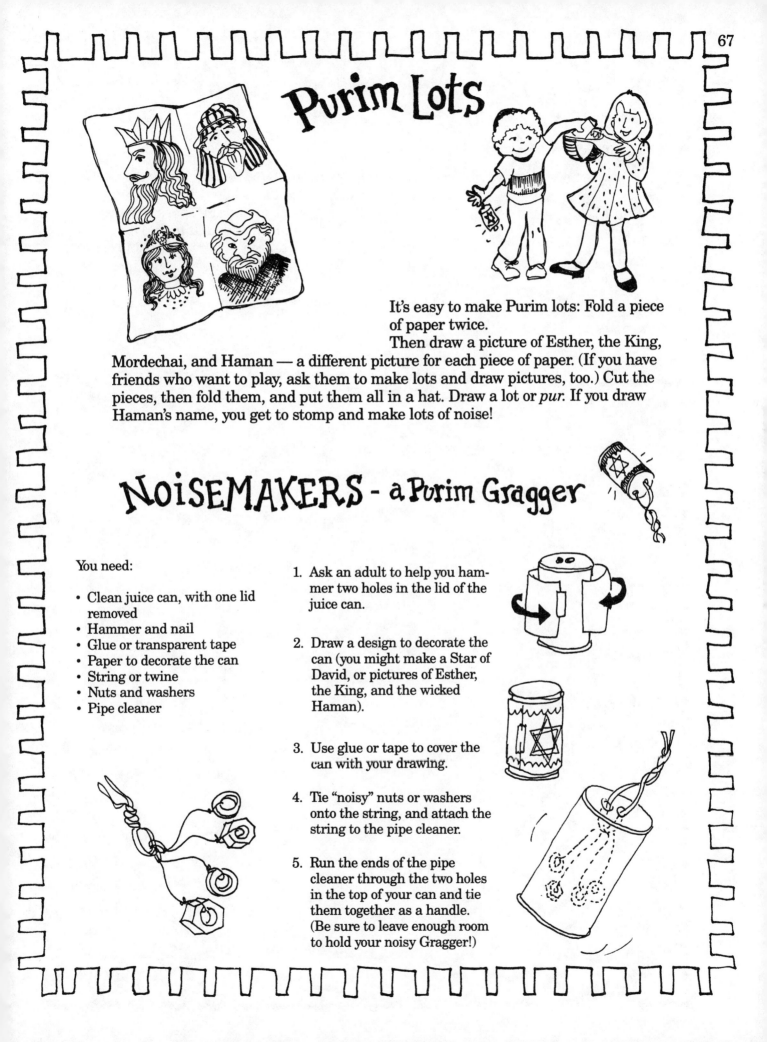

It's easy to make Purim lots: Fold a piece of paper twice.

Then draw a picture of Esther, the King, Mordechai, and Haman — a different picture for each piece of paper. (If you have friends who want to play, ask them to make lots and draw pictures, too.) Cut the pieces, then fold them, and put them all in a hat. Draw a lot or *pur*. If you draw Haman's name, you get to stomp and make lots of noise!

NoiseMAKERS - a Purim Gragger

You need:

- Clean juice can, with one lid removed
- Hammer and nail
- Glue or transparent tape
- Paper to decorate the can
- String or twine
- Nuts and washers
- Pipe cleaner

1. Ask an adult to help you hammer two holes in the lid of the juice can.

2. Draw a design to decorate the can (you might make a Star of David, or pictures of Esther, the King, and the wicked Haman).

3. Use glue or tape to cover the can with your drawing.

4. Tie "noisy" nuts or washers onto the string, and attach the string to the pipe cleaner.

5. Run the ends of the pipe cleaner through the two holes in the top of your can and tie them together as a handle. (Be sure to leave enough room to hold your noisy Gragger!)

Lucky Find

Did you know that more people of Irish descent live in the United States than in all of Ireland?

Do you know about leprechauns? The Irish tell stories about these "wee folk." Leprechauns are tiny fairies. They work very hard making shoes. They are also very rich. If you are lucky enough to find one, try to capture him. He might tell you where to find his pot of gold. Or maybe you can find it yourself in the maze.

Don't let the leprechaun trick you!

TO THE GOLD

St. Patrick's Day

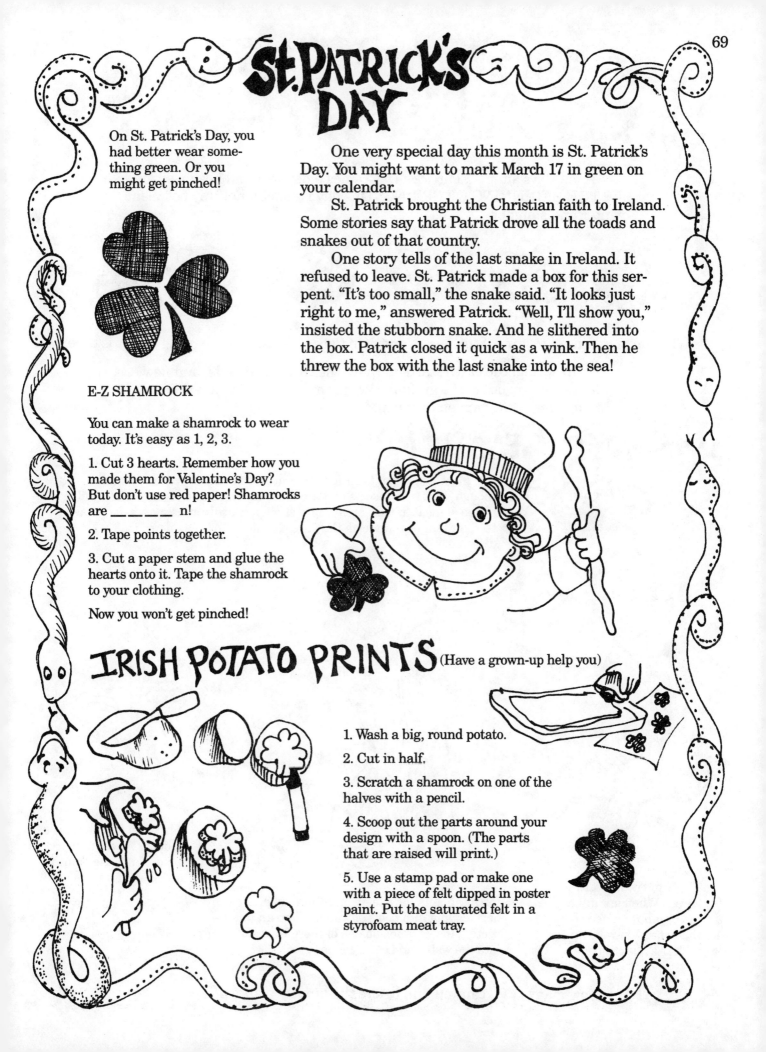

On St. Patrick's Day, you had better wear something green. Or you might get pinched!

One very special day this month is St. Patrick's Day. You might want to mark March 17 in green on your calendar.

St. Patrick brought the Christian faith to Ireland. Some stories say that Patrick drove all the toads and snakes out of that country.

One story tells of the last snake in Ireland. It refused to leave. St. Patrick made a box for this serpent. "It's too small," the snake said. "It looks just right to me," answered Patrick. "Well, I'll show you," insisted the stubborn snake. And he slithered into the box. Patrick closed it quick as a wink. Then he threw the box with the last snake into the sea!

E-Z SHAMROCK

You can make a shamrock to wear today. It's easy as 1, 2, 3.

1. Cut 3 hearts. Remember how you made them for Valentine's Day? But don't use red paper! Shamrocks are _ _ _ _ _ n!

2. Tape points together.

3. Cut a paper stem and glue the hearts onto it. Tape the shamrock to your clothing.

Now you won't get pinched!

IRISH POTATO PRINTS (Have a grown-up help you)

1. Wash a big, round potato.

2. Cut in half.

3. Scratch a shamrock on one of the halves with a pencil.

4. Scoop out the parts around your design with a spoon. (The parts that are raised will print.)

5. Use a stamp pad or make one with a piece of felt dipped in poster paint. Put the saturated felt in a styrofoam meat tray.

SPRING Things

A few days after St. Patrick's Day comes a day we've all been waiting for: THE BEGINNING OF SPRING! This day is exactly halfway between winter and summer.

What do plants need to grow? Sun, earth, and rain (lots of rain). Which spring flower is different?

In spring, the earth starts to thaw, the trees form buds, and new plants poke up out of the ground. People smile a lot. Can you think of other things that happen in spring?

BYE BYE BEASTIE!

Most plants get their food from rain and earth. There are a few plants, though, that trap insects and are meat-eating. Some of them really will eat pieces of meat, if they are hungry enough. Carnivorous plants don't have teeth or tongues. Instead, they use chemicals to break down food, so it can be digested.

These carnivorous plants grow in wet, boggy places.

The Sundew has sticky leaves. When an unlucky insect lands on one of them, the leaf rolls up with the insect inside.

Pitcher plants have leaves that form slippery tunnels leading into pools of water. When an unsuspecting insect lands on one of these leaves, it slides into the water and can't get back out.

The Venus flytrap has a mouth. When an insect lands on it, the mouth snaps shut.

How many 🕷 can you find before the hungry plants do?

Tip Toe Through The Tulips

We're lucky that the Dutch people share their tulip bulbs with other countries. How many of these beautiful flowers did you see today?

T=RED U=YELLOW L=ORANGE I=BLUE P=GREEN

Do you know why people are tired on April 1st? Because they just had a March of 31 days!

April means "to open." How many things can you think of that open in April? Color the things on this page that open.

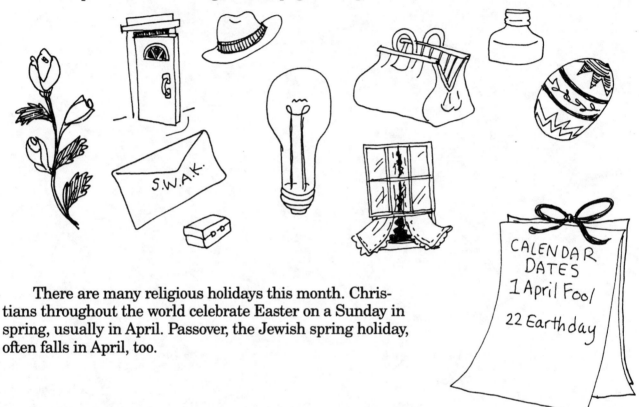

There are many religious holidays this month. Christians throughout the world celebrate Easter on a Sunday in spring, usually in April. Passover, the Jewish spring holiday, often falls in April, too.

CALENDAR DATES
1 April Fool
22 Earthday

If your 🎂 birthday is in April, your 🌿 flower is the 🌼 daisy or the 🌸 sweet pea, and the diamond is your 🐚 lucky 🦀 stone.

April Fool Feat

Turn a glass of water upside down without spilling a drop! Here's how: Fill a glass with water all the way to the top. Wet the rim. Slide a piece of cardboard across the top. Place one hand firmly on the cardboard and carefully turn the glass upside down. (Do it over the sink, just in case.) Now, take your hand away. What happens? The cardboard stays stuck to the glass, with the water still inside!

WHAT'S APRIL FOOLISH ABOUT THIS PICTURE?

You know what happens on March 32nd, of course. Everybody gets to take the day off and watch TV. It's also the day no one is allowed to eat. Happy "You Know What" Day!

74

PASSOVER

Passover is an important religious holiday that comes in spring. You can read about it in the Bible, or in a book of Bible stories (see "Some Books," at the end of this book). For Jewish people everywhere, Passover celebrates freedom.

The Old Testament tells us that the Hebrews, as the Jews were known long ago, were once slaves of the Egyptians. God sent Moses to free the Hebrews and lead them out of Egypt. And God punished the Egyptians with ten terrible plagues. Passover celebrates God's passing over the homes of the Hebrews, sparing His chosen people from punishment.

HELP THIS SHEPHERD FIND HIS WAY TO THE PROMISED LAND

Seder

Passover comes on the fifteenth day in the Hebrew month of Nisan (during March or April). Before Passover, Jewish people clean their homes, looking for bread and other foods that are not allowed on this holiday. Next they burn the bread and other forbidden foods, because they have special holiday foods to eat instead. Jewish people put away their every-day dishes and utensils, then they bring out Passover china and silverware.

The eight days of Passover begin with the Seder meal. People of the Jewish faith cook special Seder foods to remind them of their history. They roast a lamb bone and an egg as offerings at the Temple. They eat bitter herbs (like horseradish) to remember the days of slavery, and green herbs (like parsley) for the fruits of the earth. Jewish cooks also mix up a paste made from apples, nuts, and wine to represent the clay Jews made when they were slaves. And they eat flat crackers called Matzoh to remind themselves that the Hebrews left Egypt before their bread had time to rise. Then they drink to their freedom.

At the end of Seder dinner, Jewish fathers break a Matzoh and hide it. If the children find it, the father must give them a treat to get it back!

Can you find the word "Matzoh" in the others below? Look for other words about this holiday, too! (DON'T FORGET TO LOOK UP-SIDE DOWN AND BACKWARDS.)

MOSES   PHAROAH   RED SEA

FIRST BORN   SLAVE   HIDE

INDEPENDENCE   MATZOH

ANGEL   BONE   PLAGUES   SEDER

LOCUST   FREE

HOLY LAND   EGYPT   PASSOVER

```
    P A S S O V E R
 F I S R H O L Y L A N D
 B E N D E P H A R O A H T
 S R E D I D H O L B T S E S E
 E F S E A E S Z E E R F R U V
 S H E P H S O T A B E N B C O
 S H L E T P L A G U E S S O L
 T A N G E L M O S E S G L
 O C F I R S T B O R N S
 E G Y P T E V A L S
    P H I D E R
```

76

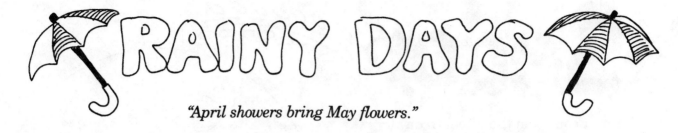

RAINY DAYS

"April showers bring May flowers."

April is often rainy. In hot regions, like much of Africa, people celebrate the new year at the beginning of the rainy season.

The Mandigo people of Sierra Leone parade to the rivers and streams. They carry water back to their villages. Then they dance and sing until the rains begin. After the rain has stopped, they plant their crops.

It's fun to play in the mud. Just make sure you don't track it in the house when you're finished!

MESSY MUD FUN in the Rain

You need:
- Mud
- Flat boards or cookie sheets
- Spade or shovel

1. With your spade or shovel, dig some dirt from the ground.
2. Mix with rain water.
3. Make into pies, patties, and animal shapes.
4. Place your creations on flat boards or cookie sheets to dry in a garage or basement.

DON'T FORGET TO CLEAN UP BEFORE GOING INSIDE.

You can also make rivers and dams.

THINGS TO DO WHEN IT RAINS!

Color the things you like to do on rainy days.

COLLECT WATER

RUN

PLAY BASEBALL

FILL A FISH BOWL

TAKE A WET WALK

HAVE A PICNIC

SPLASH IN A PUDDLE

READ A BOOK

HANG LAUNDRY

How many raindrops can you count? _____

EASTER

Easter falls on different days each year, but it is always the first Sunday following the spring full moon. The New Testament tells us about Jesus, God's son.

The Romans killed Jesus because they thought he wanted to be king. But on the Sunday after his death, his friends found Jesus' tomb empty. He appeared before them and promised that all who believed in him would live forever with God. Christians believe that those who follow Jesus Christ's teachings may die in the body, but not in the spirit. Easter, a day of rebirth, is their most important holiday.

In the spring, when Easter is celebrated, the whole world seems reborn. We see signs of life in the buds on trees, in spring flowers, and the grass that begins to turn green again. Even before Jesus was born, people celebrated the earth's rebirth every spring.

Did you know?

The Egyptians were the first people to think the rabbit was a sign of spring. Maybe that's because rabbits have lots of babies then. Here in America, there is a special Easter bunny tradition. Over 100 years ago in Fredericksburg, Texas, settlers saw Indian campfires on the night before Easter. The children were afraid, but their mother told them it was just the Easter bunny cooking eggs to bring to them. Every Easter Eve since, "rabbit fires" light the hilltops there. And children wake up to special bunny nests made from Texas wildflowers and grasses.

People from many countries (Estonia, Finland, India, Iran, Greece, Latvia, Polynesia to name a few) used to believe the earth itself was born from an egg. The egg seems like a miracle to people. It is as lifeless as a stone. But suddenly, out came a tiny baby—new life! Easter bunnies and colored eggs have been around a long, long time!

HOW MANY EGGS CAN YOU FIND ON THIS PAGE?

Easter Customs

Many of the customs
we celebrate at Easter date
back to the earliest spring festivals.

SUNRISE SERVICE

Winter was scary to early people. It was cold and dark; there was little food to eat. As days grew longer and the earth warmed up again, people held spring celebrations. They liked to get up early and watch the spring sun come up. Today, many Christians attend Easter sunrise services outdoors, rather than in church. They wait in the cool, spring darkness for the sun to rise, the way they believe Christ rose from the dead.

Did you know?

Maine is the first place in the US where the Easter sun appears. Where is the last place that Americans can see the Easter sun rise?

For hollow eggs, you need:
- Fresh eggs at room temperature
- Needle
- Paints and/or markers
- Thread
- Sturdy branch
- Marble
- Jar or vase

Shake the eggs carefully (you want to loosen the yolk, but not break the egg). Make holes, one a little larger than the other, in the ends of each raw egg. Put your lips on the smaller hole and blow the liquid out very carefully through the larger hole. Decorate hollow eggs. Thread the needle and run through the holes. Tie thread to a leafless branch. Secure the "egg tree" in a jar filled with marbles.
Hard-boiled eggs are easy to color and best for hiding!

People from the Ukraine, part of the Soviet Union, make the fanciest Easter eggs. (Copy these patterns with fine-point markers and fill in the design with tempera paints.)

How does the "bunny" send his Easter Cards?

(By Hare Mail!)

Arbor Day is a good time to celebrate all the trees in the world. Did you know that trees help keep our air and rivers clean? Where would birds live if there were no trees? What would a park look like without trees? You couldn't find any shade.

Many people in the US and Canada celebrate Arbor Day by planting trees.

FIND ALL THE THINGS MADE FROM TREES HIDDEN IN THIS PICTURE

PLANTING TREES IS EASY

1. Dig a hole in the ground twice as big as the root ball.
2. Put the tree in the hole.
3. Cover the roots with dirt and compost.
4. Pack down the soil with your feet.
5. Water every day.
6. Put your name in a bottle and plant it next to the tree. (It won't grow, but it will tell people years later that you planted this big tree.)

HAVE YOU HUGGED A TREE TODAY!

If you count the rings on the end of a tree that has been cut, you can tell how old that tree was. Each ring is one year.

April 22 is Earth Day. Millions of Americans do something special on this day to help keep our world a nice place to live. After all, it's the only home we have!

This picture is ugly. What would you do to clean it up?

Copy the picture in the space below, but take all the junk away.

May

May, the ___th month of the year, is named for the goddess of spring. It is warm, and each day is a little longer than the one before.

On the first day of May, many people celebrate the return of spring. May Day is a happy festival of flowers. In parks throughout Europe and America people put up a May Pole and hang pretty garlands from it. They dance around the pole until they can dance no more. Then they crown the May Queen with flowers.

Each of these happy May Day dancers has her own May Pole, but they've gotten their garlands mixed up. Can you tell which May Pole goes with which dancer? Use different crayons to trace the garlands.

CALENDAR DATES
1 MAY DAY
MOTHER'S DAY (2nd Sunday)
MEMORIAL DAY (4th Monday)
30 TRADITIONAL MEMORIAL DAY

May's flowers are lilies of the valley. They smell wonderful. This month's lucky gemstone is emerald. Do you know what color it is?

MAY DAY

In Ireland, people celebrate May Day by strewing flowers around the house for good luck. Some Irish farmers tie a bunch of primroses to a cow's tail.

Children in Greece have a holiday from school on May Day. Most of them spend the day picking wildflowers and making them into wreaths. Then they take the wreaths home and hang them up until June 23rd. On the evening of the 23rd, they throw the wreaths into a huge bonfire. Have you ever smelled smoke from burning flowers? Do you think it smells like perfume?

May Day in Hawaii is called Lei Day. Hawaiians are known for their friendliness. But on Lei Day, they are especially nice to each other. It is a day when nearly everyone wears a lei (say: "LAY").

Do you know what a lei is? It's a garland of flower blossoms threaded on a string and tied at the ends to form a necklace. Try making one for yourself. You'll need lots of blossoms.

Make a May Basket

You need:
- Light-colored construction paper
- Half-dollar or thread spool
- Pencil
- Scissors
- Sewing needle and thread
- Colored yarn
- Flower blossoms

1. Cut a 6" square of construction paper.
2. Fold the square diagonally (from one corner to the opposite corner).
3. With a half-dollar or spool, draw scallop shapes along the folded edge.
4. Cut around the scallops.
5. Sew the sides together with yarn to make a basket.
6. Make a handle out of yarn and attach to the basket.
7. Fill your basket with flowers.

GIVE THE BASKET TO SOMEONE YOU LIKE!

VESAK

Once upon a time there was a rich Prince in northern India. He had the best clothes, food, and fun. But all that was not enough for him. He wanted to understand life, too.

He left the palace to explore the world. Seeing so many poor and sick people, he could no longer enjoy his own good fortune. He put on tattered rags and gave up his riches. He kept only a simple bowl to beg for food. The Prince wandered far and wide, almost starving. Looking for the meaning of life, he studied with the wisest men of India. But he found no answer.

One full moon, as he was sitting under a huge tree, the Prince stopped looking *around* him. He closed his eyes and began to look *within* himself. At last, he found what he wanted. He felt a calm that he had never known before. He realized this peace exists within us all, if we will only seek it. To do so means listening to our own hearts and minds, to be content with our unique place in life. If you grow up in the Midwest, you may never have seen an ocean. You can read about it, listen to other people describe it to you, even see it in the movies or TV. But until you have visited a beach, heard the waves, smelled the sea air, seen and ridden the ocean swells, tasted the salt water, you cannot really know the ocean.

Buddha realized that all we need to know is within ourselves, just the way we learn about an ocean by visiting one. At last, the Prince understood what he wanted to know. He became "Buddha," the Enlightened One, a person who understands life.

He began to share his understanding with others. Buddha taught anyone—and everyone—who would listen, rich or poor, men or women, young or old. He taught people to know themselves if they want to understand life. And to seek a calm that comes when people stop wanting more. After all, Buddha himself only began to understand life when he stopped looking so hard for answers from others.

Help Celebrate Buddha's Birthday

Buddha's followers are called Buddhists. They live all over the world, but most are in Burma, Nepal, Japan, South Korea, Sri Lanka, Thailand, Tibet, and Vietnam. Can you find these countries on a map of Asia?

One of the Buddhists' favorite festivals, Vesak, celebrates the Prince's birth and enlightenment. Buddhists decorate their homes and temples with paper lanterns.

MAKE A PAPER LANTERN
You need:
- 9 x 12 colored construction paper
- Scissors
- Transparent tape

1. Cut 1" strip from the long side of the paper to make a handle.
2. Fold paper in half lengthwise.

3. Cut evenly spaced slits to one-half inch of the paper's edge.
4. Tape the edges together to make a cylinder.
5. Tape the handle to the inside of lantern.

Optional: Decorate your construction paper with crayons or markers before cutting.

In Laos, people have a rocket festival. Each village and temple builds its own rocket, decorating it with flowers and streamers. The village whose rocket goes the farthest on Buddha's Birthday is considered the best.

CLAY

MAKE A ROCKET
You need:
- Soft plastic bottle (dishwashing liquid bottle is ok)
- Knife **(with a grown-up to help you)**
- 2 straws (one narrower than the other)
- Modeling clay
- Paper
- Glue

1. With the sharp point of a knife, cut a hole in the bottle's cap that is just big enough for the smaller straw. (Or ask a grown-up to do this.)

2. Attach this straw firmly to the cap with clay.
3. Cut about 4 inches off the larger straw, and decorate one end with two paper triangles.
4. Make a nose for the other end of the larger straw with modeling clay. (If the nose is round, no one can get hurt.)
5. Slide the larger "rocket" straw onto the smaller one. Squeeze the plastic bottle and make the rocket fly!

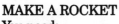

What makes your rocket "fly"? (Have you ever blown the paper wrapper off a straw?)

HOORAY for MOMS

Mother's Day is when we thank our moms for all they have done for us. Draw a big heart around all the things your mother has done for you. Then color the pictures below.

Where would we be without our mothers? (Still not born!)

Happy Mother's Day Presents

Nothing makes a hard-working mother happier than when a child she loves does something nice for her!

Breakfast in bed is a special treat for Moms the world over. If you ask your father and brother or sister to help, it can also be fun!

Here's an easy breakfast to make your mother:

EGG IN A NEST

You need:

- Slice of bread (your Mom's favorite kind)
- Two-inch cookie or biscuit cutter (a glass will always do)
- Large skillet with a cover
- Butter or margarine
- 1 egg

1. Cut a circle in the middle of the bread. (You can eat the circle, if you get hungry making your mother's breakfast.)
2. Put the skillet on stove, and melt the butter or margarine over medium heat.
3. Add bread and brown on one side.
4. Flip bread and lower heat.

5. Break an egg into the hole in the bread. (You can ask someone for help doing this, if you want.)
6. Cover the frying pan and cook until the egg begins to firm. (Ask your family how Mom likes her egg: 3 minutes cooks an egg soft; 5 minutes cooks an egg hard.)

Serve with fresh fruit or juice, hot coffee (only fill Mom's cup halfway—she'd feel sad if you burned yourself carrying it), and a big hug!

Another nice Mother's Day present is a book of coupons that your Mom can use when she needs them.

MOM'S LOVE COUPON BOOK

You need:
- 3 x 5 cards
- Pencil or pen
- Hole punch
- Ribbon or thick yarn

Think of all the things you can do to make your mother happy (pick up toys, be nice to your sister or brother, water plants, clear the table, wash dishes, etc.) and write or draw a picture of each chore on a "coupon." Stack all the cards together with an extra one on top. Then punch holes through all of them. Tie together with ribbon or yarn. Decorate the blank "cover" card and give the coupon book to your Mom.

MEMORIAL DAY

Memorial Day is always the last Monday in May. Grown-ups don't go to work. Kids have a day off school. Some people think of this holiday as the beginning of summer. (How many days are there before summer officially begins?)

Memorial Day began as a way to remember the brave soldiers who fought in the American Civil War. All wars are terrible, because people are hurt and many die. But the Civil War was especially sad, because Americans fought other Americans. In some places, like Maryland and Virginia, brother fought brother. In southern states where the war mostly took place, cities and homes were ruined.

When the Civil War ended, a New York druggist, Henry Welles, saw the soldiers returning home. He was happy the war was over, but felt sad for all the people who had been hurt. "We must do something for the soldiers who risked their lives," he thought. He decided to organize a big celebration.

People liked the druggist's idea. Throughout the country, Americans began to celebrate Memorial Day. They held parades and picnic suppers. In the Northern states people put US flags on soldiers' graves. Southerners put flowers on soldiers' graves.

We have lost many more Americans in wars since the Civil War. Today, we honor all those who died protecting our country. And we think hard about ways to make peace, instead of more wars. Can you think of any? (Home is good place to practice making peace.)

Make A Memorial Day Poppy

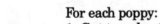

For each poppy:
1. Cut two sheets of tissue in quarters.

2. Fold pieces of paper lengthwise, like an accordian.

You need:
• Tissue paper, 20" x 30" (two shades of red or pink)
• Scissors
• Green "twist-ems" from a box of plastic bags

3. Tie together with "twist-ems."

⭐ CELEBRATE WITH A PARADE

Parades are a fun way to celebrate Memorial Day – or Independence and Veterans' Day! You can have a parade any day you want – all you need are musical instruments and some friends to march with.

To Beat: You can make a drum out of all sorts of things (an empty coffee can and an empty plastic milk jug work well).

Use a pencil with an eraser as a drum stick, or put a metal nut on one end to make a different sound.

To Strum: Put a rubber band around a book. Then slide a paper cup underneath the rubber band. Pluck the "string." Do you get different sounds if you move the cup around? (Try near the end of the book and then in the middle.)

To Chime or Ring: Sew bells onto a ribbon, then tie it to your arm or leg for easy marching "music."

Even bolts, nails, and screws will chime, if you tie them together on a coat hanger.

Or Quietly Ping: Hold a fork on a plastic lid of an empty can. Then ping the prongs with your fingernails to hear this "instrument" sing.

To Toot: Wrap wax paper over a comb. Hold comb lightly against your lips and hum.

To Shake or Rattle: Fill an empty milk carton or dish detergent bottle with dry beans or gravel. Or tie old keys together with string (be sure to ask you parents to give you keys they don't need). Then **Roll** your marching band off in parade formation!

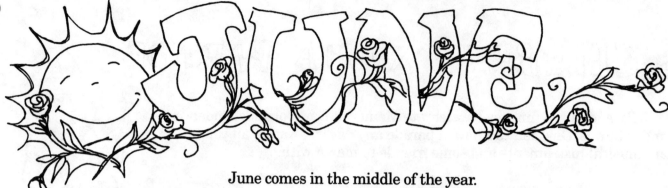

June comes in the middle of the year.
It is month number ____ . Do you know what's special about June 21st?
It's the first day of summer! Do you know something else special about
that day? It's the longest day of the year. The 21st is the day to do your
favorite thing outside because it won't get dark until late. If you like to
hike, this would be the best day to do it.

Were you born in June? If so, your flower would be the rose. Your lucky gemstones
would be pearls or agates.

```
M L P A R H X Z W N T F
E A C B P T M S O O P E
F J P R S R J D C G C B
R X D U V N I Q T B A R
I C G E E O P L O E X U
D U N A C V I H B L D A
A S E P T E M B E R Y R
Y K J G I M M A R C H Y
T C U J H E A B D F D N
J A N U A R Y L E T P E
O B E L M T O N Y R O J
H G N Y F H I C X E F B
M L N O V E M B E R S F
```

Can you find JUNE hidden in
these letters? All the other
months and one weekday are
here too. Circle the ones you find.
Look up, down, sideways, and
diagonally.

- January
- February
- March
- April
- May
- June
- July
- August
- September
- October
- November
- December

- Friday

"Marry when June roses grow,
Over land and sea you'll go."

CALENDAR DATES
14 FLAG DAY
21 BEGINNING OF SUMMER
LAST DAY OF SCHOOL!

JUNE WEDDING

Why do more people get married in June than any other month? Maybe it's because the weather is perfect—a good way to start a life of togetherness!

Wedding customs are as ancient as many of our holidays. People used to think that throwing rice at the bride and groom after the wedding would help them have many children. They still throw rice, but it doesn't mean the couple will have a big family.

In the United States, pioneer women would give a "pounding" party for a new bride. It was called that because each woman would give a pound of food. What kind of food do you think they might give?

According to custom, good luck will come to brides who wear something old, something new, something borrowed, and something blue. Can you think of some things the bride might wear?

Did you know in some countries parents choose who their children will marry? In parts of Africa, a groom must pay the bride's father before they can get married. The price is usually a herd of cattle.

WEDDING GIFTS

Can you guess what's inside these gifts by their shapes and the clues in the facts above?

ARABIAN HAND-PAINTING

In Arab countries, brides often paint fancy patterns on their hands so they will look beautiful for their weddings. You can try it with poster paints. Can you copy these designs?

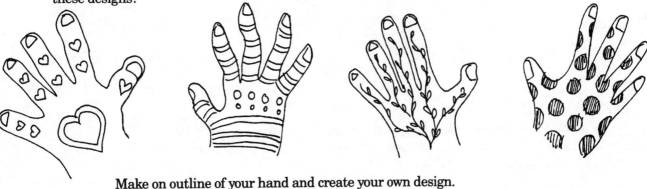

Make on outline of your hand and create your own design.

FLAG DAY

An American flag flew over a hill near Boston, Massachusetts when George Washington led colonial troops against British soldiers. It had 13 red and blue stripes for the 13 American colonies, as well as crosses for St. Andrew and St. George of Great Britain. Until July 4, 1776, America remained part of Britain. (You can read more about the first Independence Day on page 103.)

After the Declaration of Independence, Americans wanted their very own flag – without any reminder of Britain. A Pennsylvania woman, Betsy Ross, who was very clever with needle and thread, may have sewed the first real American flag. It had red and white stripes with white stars on a field of blue. After the Revolution, the American Congress passed a law that every time a new state joined the Union a new star would be added to our flag. So there have been a lot of different flags since the first Flag Day in 1777!

Color Old Glory below. How many states have joined the Union since Betsy Ross made the first US flag with its thirteen stars?

Do You Know?

I pledge allegiance to the flag of the United States of America and to the Republic for which it stands, one nation under God, indivisible, with liberty and justice for all.

OTHER FLAGS

The first flags appeared in China, but it was the Arabs who brought them to Europe. Early flags were probably just pieces of cloth tied onto sticks or poles. The Aztec Indians in Mexico used flags made of feathers. They also attached flags to soldiers' backs.

Every nation in the world has its very own flag—and many have changed, much the way the American flag has. But international flags are important, too. They help people from many different countries to speak the same language.

ALPHABET FLAGS

☐ WHITE ▨ YELLOW   ▦ RED ▥ BLUE ■ BLACK

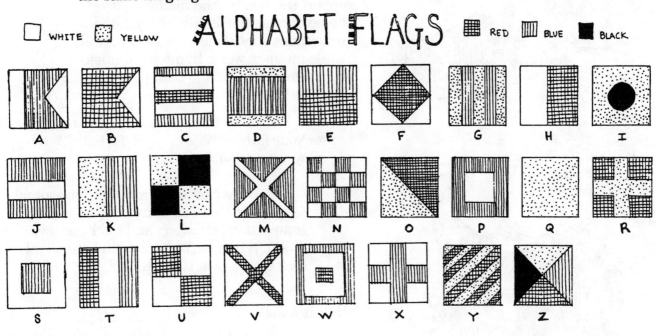

Can you "read" this message?

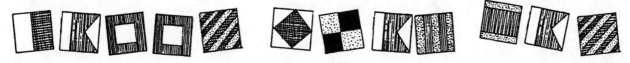

MAKE YOUR OWN FLAG

You need:
- 12" square from an old white pillowcase or sheet
- Scissors and tape
- Crayons
- Newspaper/construction paper
- Iron **(with an adult's permission or help)**
- White glue
- 1/4" dowel, about 2' long

1. Tape cloth to work table or counter top.

2. Crayon a design on your flag. (Create your own or copy one of the flags on these pages.)
3. Crayon a second layer, so wax is thick.
4. Place cloth on old paper layers, and cover with a clean piece of construction paper.

5. Ask a grown-up to iron these layers, or to show you how.

6. Cover 12" of the dowel with glue. Roll one end of your flag once around the dowel and squeeze tight.
7. Let dry, then fly!

Do you know what a white flag means?

What about this flag?

Different Dads

This is the day you do something special for your father. What surprise are you planning for him?

Fathers are very important. Mothers carry and bear babies, but without a father, there would be no baby in the first place!

It used to be that fathers went out to work to support the family. And mothers stayed home to raise the family. Today, fathers sometimes stay home to raise the family, while mothers work. In many families, both parents work, and both parents raise their children.

Who fixes your breakfast? Your mother or your father? Who gives you a bath? Who plays games with you?

Fathers can be as important in animal families as they are in human ones. With some animals, fathers and mothers have different names. Write the kind of animal each father is in the blanks.

A father is a male ____ ____ ____ ____ ____
M U H A N

A buck is a male ____ ____ ____ ____
E D E R

A ram is a male ____ ____ ____ ____ ____
P H E E S

A drake is a male ____ ____ ____ ____ ____
S O G O E

A sire is a male ____ ____ ____ ____ ____
R E H S O

FATHER'S DAY

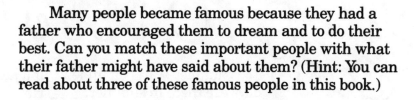

Many people became famous because they had a father who encouraged them to dream and to do their best. Can you match these important people with what their father might have said about them? (Hint: You can read about three of these famous people in this book.)

Neil Armstrong   Esther   Martin Luther King

Sandra Day O'Connor

I taught my daugher to ride and let her swim in the water tank on our ranch. She became the first woman to serve on the US Supreme Court.

— — — — — — — —   — — — — — — — —

My son became a minister like me, but he also led the struggle for civil rights, won a Nobel Prize for Peace, and has a national holiday celebrated on his birthday.

— — — — — — — —   — — — — — — — —

She called me "Uncle," but I tried to be a father to this orphan. As queen of Persia, my "daughter" repaid me by saving my life—and the lives of all our people.

— — — — — —

When my son was only three, I took him to watch the air races in Cleveland, Ohio. He loved planes so much it was no wonder he built the best models and had a pilot's license by 16. But even I was surprised that he would be the first man to set foot on the moon!

— — — — — — —   — — — — — — — — —

MAKE A PICTURE FRAME TO REMIND YOUR DAD OF SOMEONE WHO MAY BE FAMOUS ONE DAY (You, of course!)

You need:
- 2 cups flour
- 1 cup salt
- 5 cups water
- Large mixing bowl
- Your picture
- Water
- Waxed paper
- Paper clips and fork
- Paint brush and watered-down white glue

1. Mix flour, salt, and water in a bowl.
2. Make a ball the size of a baseball, then divide it equally into four parts. (Save the rest of the clay, in case you make a mistake, or to have for other projects. Put extra clay in a plastic bag and seal tightly.)
3. Lay each part onto a piece of waxed paper and roll into log shapes. Flatten them with your thumbs. You want your picture to fit inside these four pieces of frame.

4. Use a little water to "glue" the four corners together.
5. Decorate your frame with designs from paper clips or the tines of a fork.
6. Bake frame on an old cookie sheet in a 350 degree oven for one hour.

7. Brush on glue that is the consistency of poster paint. When this is dry, tape your picture to the back of the frame. And give to your proud Dad!

Summer

Summer starts on June 21 and lasts until September 21. How many days are there in summer?____ How many months?____ Do you think it is long enough?

During this season the top half of the earth tilts toward the sun. That's why summer can be hot. It's also the time of year when the top half of the world gets more sunlight, so the days are long.

GARDEN FRESH VEGGIES

Summer is the time of year to eat vegetables fresh from the garden. What parts of plants do we eat? Draw a line from the part to the correct picture. Then, unscramble the name.

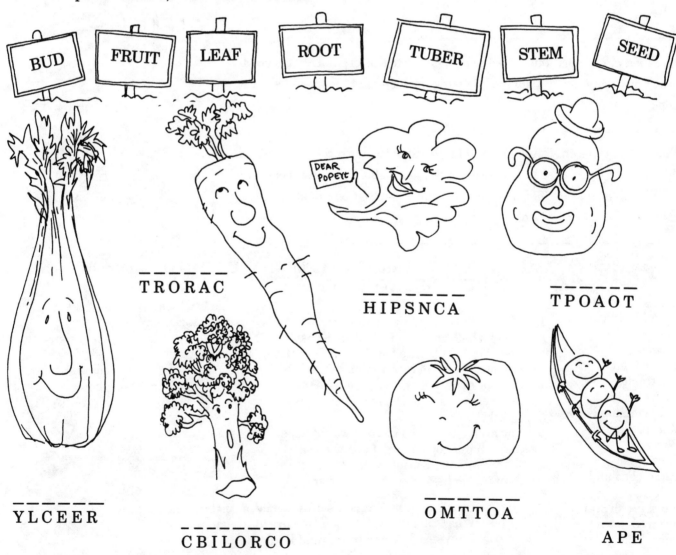

BUD   FRUIT   LEAF   ROOT   TUBER   STEM   SEED

DEAR POPEYE

_ _ _ _ _ _
T R O R A C

_ _ _ _ _ _ _
H I P S N C A

_ _ _ _ _ _
T P O A O T

_ _ _ _ _
Y L C E E R

_ _ _ _ _ _ _ _
C B I L O R C O

_ _ _ _ _
O M T T O A

_ _ _
A P E

HOW MANY "SUMMER REMINDERS" CAN YOU "HOOK"?

JUICY ICE POPS

If you're hot, make some "juicy ice pops" to cool down.

1. Pour fruit juice into small paper cups.

2. Put the cups in the freezer.

3. When the juice has started to harden, put popsicle sticks in the middle of each cup.

4. When the juice is completely frozen, run the cups briefly under warm water. Then pop the "juicy ice pops" out of the cups and ENJOY!

BREAKING THE FAST

Muslims the world over celebrate the end of a long fast in the summer, usually near the end of June. Ramadan, this Islamic fast, is a little like the Christians' Lent. Breaking the fast lasts for three days, beginning with a large prayer ceremony at a mosque (say MOSK). Then people have parties, exchange gifts, and give candy or money to children.

In Turkey, this celebration is known as "Candy Holiday," because kids get handkerchiefs filled with candies and coins. In the Sudan, children receive red candy dolls. Muslim children in Pakistan enjoy *sawaeen,* sweet noodles made from dates, flour, milk, nuts, and sugar.

~ HOW TO MAKE TURKISH CANDY ~

You need:
- 1/4 cup orange juice
- 1 package unflavored gelatin
- 1 package lemon or orange Jello
- 1 cup sugar
- 1 cup hot water
- **and a grown-up to help you!**

PLUS A JELLY THERMOMETER

1. Put a square baking pan in the refrigerator while you make candy.
2. Dissolve unflavored gelatin in orange juice.
3. Mix Jello, sugar, and hot water in a deep, heavy-bottomed saucepan. Heat, stirring until mixture starts to boil. Put candy or jelly thermometer into the pan and cook until temperature reaches 222 degrees.
4. Remove pan from stove and add softened gelatin and orange juice.
5. Let mixture cool. Then pour into cool baking pan. Put back in refrigerator until syrup is stiff and firm (about two hours).

6. Sprinkle sugar on a piece of aluminum foil or wax paper.
7. Run a knife under hot water. Then use it to loosen edges of stiff candy.
8. Run hot water in sink and dip the bottom of the pan into the water for just one minute to loosen the candy.
9. Put the candy on paper or foil and sprinkle more sugar on top.
10. Cut the candy into small pieces and roll in leftover sugar.
11. Store what you can't eat in a cool, dry place.

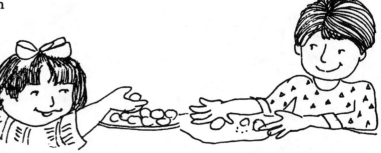

What Do You Know About Islam?

Islam is one of the world's most important religions. Look at the map on the next page at all the countries where Muslims live.

Like Christians and Jews, Muslims worship only one God. They believe in the teachings of their Prophets, people like Moses and Jesus, but especially Muhammed. Muhammed was a trader and a camel-driver, an important job in the Middle East 1500 years ago. People respected and trusted him. Muslims believe that an angel brought the word of God to Muhammed and told him to spread God's message to others.

Today, Muslim children learn the Koran in Arabic, no matter what language they speak. Muslims believe the Koran holds all the rules people need to live by and that it must be obeyed without question. Faithful Muslims try to visit Mecca, their holy city in Saudi Arabia, at least once in their lives. Over 2,000,000 people visit Mecca every year.

99

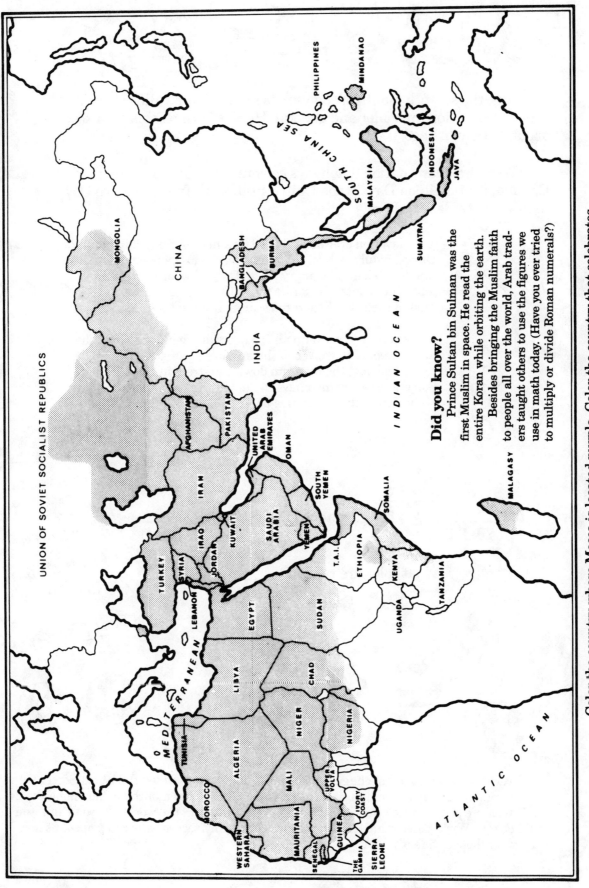

Color the country where Mecca is located purple. Color the country that celebrates "Candy Holiday" yellow. Color India's Muslim neighbors orange. Color all the Muslim countries in Africa blue. (Don't forget the island nation.) Color the Soviet Muslims red. Color the Muslim countries in Southeast Asia green.

Did you know?

Prince Sultan bin Sulman was the first Muslim in space. He read the entire Koran while orbiting the earth.

Besides bringing the Muslim faith to people all over the world, Arab traders taught others to use the figures we use in math today. (Have you ever tried to multiply or divide Roman numerals?)

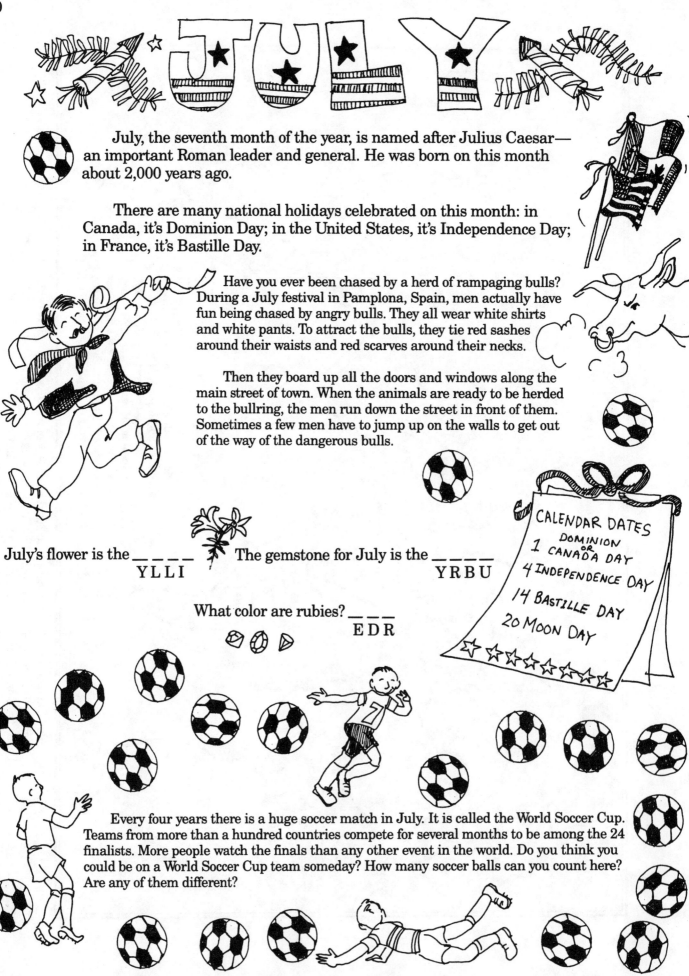

JULY

July, the seventh month of the year, is named after Julius Caesar—an important Roman leader and general. He was born on this month about 2,000 years ago.

There are many national holidays celebrated on this month: in Canada, it's Dominion Day; in the United States, it's Independence Day; in France, it's Bastille Day.

Have you ever been chased by a herd of rampaging bulls? During a July festival in Pamplona, Spain, men actually have fun being chased by angry bulls. They all wear white shirts and white pants. To attract the bulls, they tie red sashes around their waists and red scarves around their necks.

Then they board up all the doors and windows along the main street of town. When the animals are ready to be herded to the bullring, the men run down the street in front of them. Sometimes a few men have to jump up on the walls to get out of the way of the dangerous bulls.

July's flower is the _ _ _ _   The gemstone for July is the _ _ _ _
YLLI   YRBU

What color are rubies? _ _ _
EDR

CALENDAR DATES
1 DOMINION OR CANADA DAY
4 INDEPENDENCE DAY
14 BASTILLE DAY
20 MOON DAY

Every four years there is a huge soccer match in July. It is called the World Soccer Cup. Teams from more than a hundred countries compete for several months to be among the 24 finalists. More people watch the finals than any other event in the world. Do you think you could be on a World Soccer Cup team someday? How many soccer balls can you count here? Are any of them different?

Knee High by the 4th of July

This is a verse that American farmers often say. It means if their corn is as high as their knees by early July, they will have a good crop. How high is the corn where you live on the 4th of July?

CAN YOU MATCH THE FARMER WITH HIS KNEE HIGH CORN STALK? (PUT THE LETTER BY THE CORN.)

Independence Days

In July, many countries celebrate their freedom. Canadians celebrate on July 1 with parades and picnics. On this day in 1867, the British colonies in North America became a Dominion, run by their own Parliament. On Dominion Day, you can see the famous Mounted Police, wearing their bright red jackets.

The French celebrate Bastille Day on July 14. Besides parades and fireworks, Bastille Day is famous for parties at fire stations. Two hundred years ago, the people of Paris stormed the Bastille prison. Then the people, rather than the king, began to govern. Today on Bastille Day, French firemen serve dinner and make music for everyone to enjoy.

In South America, people celebrate the birthday of Simon Bolivar on July 24. He led soldiers across 10 rivers during the rainy season and up the Andes, some of the highest mountains in the world. Forcing the Spanish to leave South America, Bolivar and his men won freedom for Bolivia, Ecuador, Peru, and Venezuela.

On the next page, you can read how American colonists declared their independence from the "Mother Country," Great Britain. Washington, DC is a good place to celebrate America's Independence Day.

Can you find the countries mentioned above on this map? Put a star on the ones that celebrate their freedom this month. Do you see a person who reminds you of each country's Independence Day? Draw a line from the person who best represents each nation to that country. If a new nation broke away from another country, draw a dotted line connecting the old government with the new.

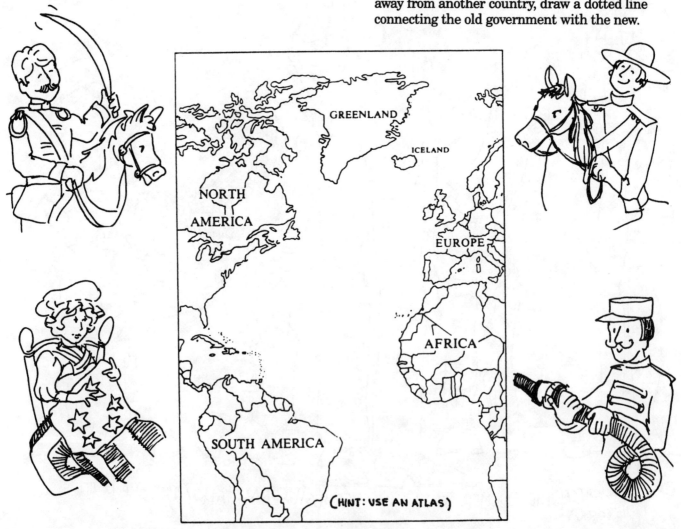

GREENLAND

ICELAND

NORTH AMERICA

EUROPE

AFRICA

SOUTH AMERICA

(HINT: USE AN ATLAS)

The Fourth of July

July 4, 1776 the thirteen American colonies declared their independence from Great Britain. Each colony sent representatives to Philadelphia. Richard Henry Lee of Virginia said that the colonies should be "free and independent states." Massachusetts' John Adams seconded Lee's motion, but some of the delegates hesitated to take such a bold step.

ROBERT LIVINGSTON
Ben Franklin
THOMAS JEFFERSON
John Adams
ROGER SHERMAN

Five men were chosen to justify independence. Their pictures are to the left. Thomas Jefferson did most of the writing, but John Hancock, President of Congress, signed first (his is the largest signature).

Find the signatures of the Committee who worked on the Declaration of Independence. Which member of the Committee did not sign?

Benj. Franklin   John Adams

Roger Sherman

Th Jefferson

Which signer had the most unusual name: Delaware's Caesar Rodney, Georgia's Button Gwinnett, or Massachusetts' Elbridge Gerry?

Make "John Hancock's Quill Pen"

You need:
- Ball point pen
- Construction paper
- Scissors
- Transparent tape

John Hancock

To make your own "John Hancock," use a 'pretend' quill.

1. Roll paper around a pen. Leave the tip free, so you can write your signature.
2. Cut the paper wide enough to wrap around the pen. Tape it securely.
3. Cut a triangle from the paper you have left to fit onto the pen.
4. Cut the slant of the triangle to look like a feather, and tape to the pen.

PRACTICE YOUR "JOHN HANCOCK" BELOW:

1. Print or write your name in cursive.
2. With a pen, thicken one side of each letter (but not top or bottom).
3. Add curly thin lines from ends of the letters.
4. Keep practicing (look at signature above).

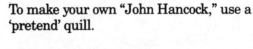

John   Mary

John & Mary

_____

_____

MOON DAY

This astronaut needs to return to his landing module in 20 steps.
Draw a line through the maze to show his route.

On July 20, 1969, a very special event happened.
Not here on earth, but on the moon! This was the
day that astronaut Neil Armstrong put the first
human footprint on the moon. Do you think that
footprint is still there? After reading the facts below,
you might come up with the right answer.

MOON FACTS

- The moon is our closest neighbor in space—
  250,000 miles, or three days by spaceship. The
  next closest neighbor is Venus, 100 times farther
  away.
- You can see the moon because it reflects the sun's
  light.
- The earth is four times as big as the moon. If the
  earth were the size of a basketball, the moon would
  equal the size of a baseball.

- On the part of the moon we can see, it gets hot
  enough for water to boil. (How hot is that? 212
  degrees.) On the dark side of the moon, it can get
  as cold as 320 degrees below zero.
- There is no life on the moon. There is no air, no
  water, no wind, not even any sound.
- There are mountains and craters on the moon.
  They make shadows, and give the "Man in the
  Moon" his "face."
- You could jump six times higher on the moon than
  on earth, because there is less gravity on the moon.

SUMMER VACATION

How many days does your summer vacation last? You can count the days on your calendar. Start with the last day of school in June and keep counting to the first day of school in September.

1. Days in June _____

2. Minus date of last day of school _ _____

3. Total vacation days in June _____

4. Days in July + _____

5. Days in August + _____

6. Day school starts in September + _____

TOTAL _____

If you know how to add and subtract, there is a short cut. How many days are in June? Subtract the date school gets out from that number. How many days are in July? How many in August? What date does school begin in September? Add steps 3-6 and you will know exactly how long your vacation is.

If you know how to divide, you can also tell how many weeks your vacation lasts. Just divide the total days by 7. (If the number of days doesn't divide evenly, you might end up with a few extra days.)

HOW MANY NUMBERS CAN YOU FIND IN THIS SUMMER VACATION PICTURE?

0's ____ 1's ____ 2's ____ 3's ____ 4's ____ 5's ____ 6's ____ 7's ____ 8's ____ 9's ____

106

Summer Vacation Travel

Are you going away this summer? Where? On this map of the United States, color all the states you plan to visit this vacation in red. Color the ones you've been to before in yellow. Any states that you visit more than once will come out ___ ___ ___ ___ ___ ___ .

N E G R O A

How far will you travel on your vacation? You can figure it out, if you know how to multiply. Using a ruler, measure the distance from the edge of the state where you start to the edge of the state where you will end up. A half inch equals 150 miles. One inch equals 300 miles. How many miles will you travel? Is that one-way or round-trip?

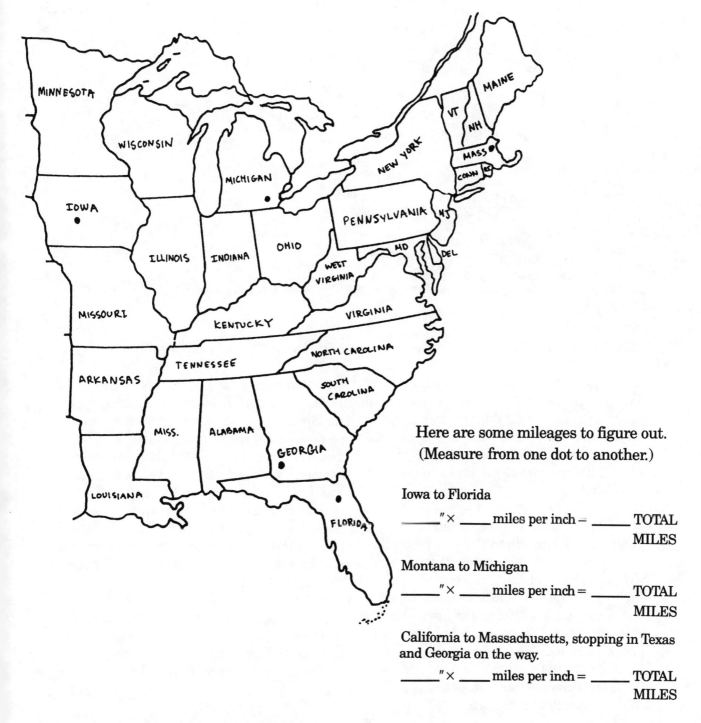

Here are some mileages to figure out.
(Measure from one dot to another.)

Iowa to Florida

_____" × _____ miles per inch = _____ TOTAL MILES

Montana to Michigan

_____" × _____ miles per inch = _____ TOTAL MILES

California to Massachusetts, stopping in Texas and Georgia on the way.

_____" × _____ miles per inch = _____ TOTAL MILES

(Note: if you are measuring from one page to the other, stop at the edge of the last state on one page, and start measuring from the edge of the next state on the other page.)

CLOUDS and THUNDERSTORMS

Summertime is a good time to look at clouds. Many are big and puffy. They look like ice cream cones or mashed potatoes—or sometimes animals. Puffy clouds are called cumulus (CUME-u-luss) clouds. Thunderstorms come from the biggest, tallest cumulus clouds. These are called cumulonimbus clouds. Nimbus means "black" in Latin.

What is a Cloud?

When you boil water, what happens? The hot, moist air from the pot rises. (The water **evaporates.**) When it meets cooler air, it forms into water droplets again. (It **condenses.**) The condensed air is called steam. Steam is really a small cloud in your kitchen.

Clouds start as water from oceans, lakes and rivers. When the sun heats this water, some of it evaporates. It floats up through the sky like a balloon. The air high up in the sky is always cold. When the warm, evaporated water rises into this cold air, it turns into water droplets again and becomes a cloud. Clouds are really a lot of steam in the sky. When clouds become too full of water, big, heavy drops fall to the ground. This is rain.

What is a Thunderstorm?

Sometimes on hot summer afternoons, moist air from the ground rushes up through the sky very quickly. It rises so fast that it rubs with raindrops falling down. The rubbing, or **friction**, makes electricity. The electricity makes a huge spark. This is called lightning.

The lightning heats the air so fast that the air rushes out of the cloud with a bang. That's thunder. When air rushes out of a broken balloon, it makes a loud noise, much like thunder.

Where's the safest place to be in a thunderstorm? In a building with a metal frame or in a car. Don't stand under a tree. It attracts lightning. And stay away from water. It also attracts lightning.

LOOK UP

Clouds are filled with wondrous, ever-changing shapes. Can you imagine these animals when you look at clouds?

Can you find eight animals? Color them different colors.

110

The eighth month of the year is named after another Roman Caesar: Augustus.

If you have a garden, you'll know why the English sometimes call August, "Weed Month." Do you know what a weed is? It is a plant that's not wanted where it is growing.

August is the month when many farmers harvest their crops. They have a rhyme:

"We've ploughed, we've sowed,
We've reaped, we've mowed,
We've got our harvest in."

Can you put these pictures in the right order to go with the rhyme above?
Write a number under each box to show the order of events.

A VEGETABLE WITH YOUR NAME ON IT

Scratch your name on a small pumpkin, zucchini, or gourd that's still growing in the garden. When it grows bigger and is ready to pick in the fall, it will be your own personalized vegetable.

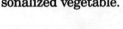

CALENDAR DATES
"UN BIRTHDAY"
CLOWN WEEK
1ST WEEK IN AUGUST
SHOOTING STARS
11-12

August's flowers are gladioli. This month has two gemstones: the sardonyx is brownish; the carnelian is bright red.

Summer Olympics

Every fourth year in August there is an important event for athletes around the world: the Summer Olympics. More than 160 countries have teams that compete in the Olympics. The team that wins an event gets a gold medal. The second place team gets a silver medal. The third place team gets a bronze medal.

This competition started more than 2,700 years ago in ancient Greece. The Greeks had some of the same sports we have today—boxing, wrestling, javelin and discus throwing, foot races, and jumping. But in the first Olympics games they also had chariot races and contests for poets, orators, and playwrights.

Some of the equipment Olympic athletes use are hidden in this picture. Put a circle around the ones you can find.

Diving • Archery • Basketball • Boxing • Canoeing • Swimming

Pole Vault • Hammer • Discus • Shot Put • Javelin

Equestrian (Horseback Riding) • Fencing • Weight Lifting

Track shoes • Hurdles • High Jump • Yachting • Cycling

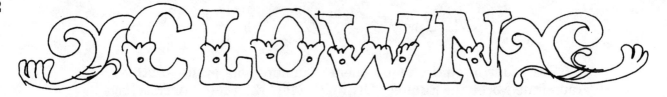

CLOWN

If you have ever been to a circus, you know that clowns are always around to make you laugh. The time to celebrate clowns is in August, during Clown Week.

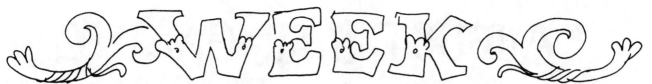

These funny people come in all shapes and sizes. They dress in outlandish costumes, and paint crazy designs on their faces.

No two clowns look exactly alike, except in these coloring pictures. Can you find the twins? Color them exactly the same.

AUGUST STAR GAZING

Summer is a fun time for star-gazing. You can also see meteors this season. They are so common in August that one night, usually August 11 or 12, is known as the Night of the Shooting Stars. Some scientists have been able to see as many as 60 meteors an hour then.

Did you know that meteors aren't shooting stars at all? They are really bits of dust or rock – some no bigger than one of your fingernails. Even though they may be very tiny, they glow brightly as they enter earth's atmosphere. That's because meteors travel very fast – faster than a bullet from a gun. And they rub up against other tiny particles in the air. What happens when you rub your hands together? Multiply that by the speed meteors travel, and all the particles they rub up against. Then maybe you can see how something very small can produce so bright a light!

The best place to look for meteors is the constellation Perseus. (A constellation is a collection of stars that form a pattern.) Look for Perseus in the northern part of the Milky Way.

Do you know how to find the North Star? Once you know where it is, you can never lose your sense of direction – at least not on a starry night! Whenever you face the North Star, you are also facing North. To find it, look up in the sky for the Big Dipper. Then draw an imaginary line from the cup of this dipper until you come to the handle of the smaller dipper. The North Star is at the end of the handle in the Little Dipper.

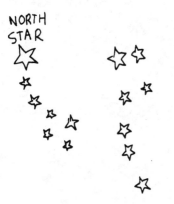

NORTH STAR

Asians tell a story about two stars we see in August. They say that a peasant played his flute so well that a heavenly princess left the skies to hear him. The Weaver Princess, Vega, fell in love with the peasant, named Altair. So they married.

When the Queen of Heaven found her daughter's loom empty, she brought Vega back. But because her daughter was so unhappy without her husband, the Queen allowed Altair to join them in the heavens. He flew like an eagle to reach his bride (maybe that's why his constellation looks like this bird).

To keep her daughter hard at work, the Queen of Heaven drew a line of stars (the Silver River or the Milky Way) to separate the couple. But she allowed Vega and Altair one night to visit each other. Once a year, on the seventh night of the seventh moon, Vega and Altair are reunited. Look at these "lover" stars August 6 – 10.

PERSEUS · CASSIOPEIA · DENEB · VEGA · ALTAIR

The North Star is very special. It is the only star in the sky that doesn't move with the seasons.

★ ✩ SEEING STARS ✩ ★

☆ The Romans thought each person had his or her own star in heaven. To them a falling star meant that someone had died.

☆ Some people like to make a wish when they see a meteor.

☆ Escaped slaves used to look for the Big and Little Dipper to guide them North.

☆ Native Americans thought of these stars as Big Bear and Little Bear.

Connect the dots to see what early peoples imagined in the night sky years ago.

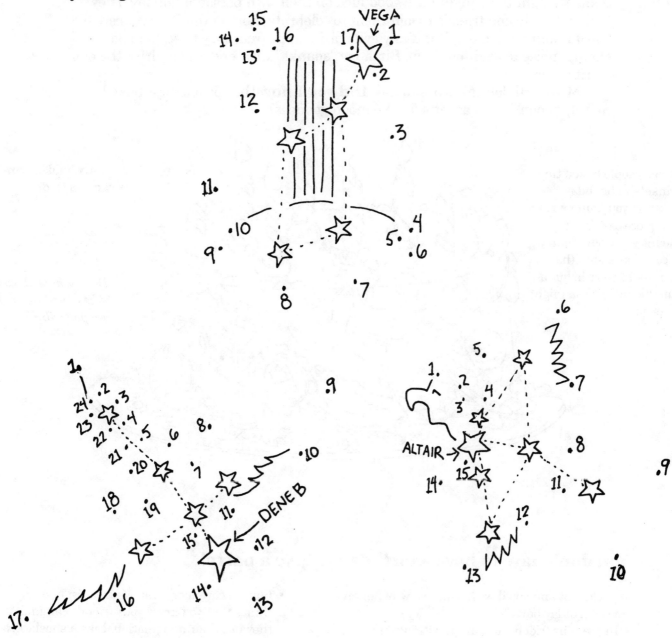

Did you know the night sky is different, depending what time of year you look up at the stars? H. A. Rey's *Find the Constellations* is a good way to learn more about how constellations move through the seasons.

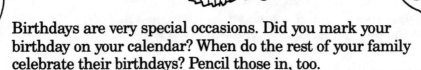

Birthdays are very special occasions. Did you mark your birthday on your calendar? When do the rest of your family celebrate their birthdays? Pencil those in, too.

Before people invented calendars, they had no way of remembering birthdays. Many humans never even knew how old they were!

Only after calendars were used, did people begin to celebrate birthdays. Some thought they might have good luck on their own personal holiday. They invited family and friends to join them to celebrate, hoping that happy, festive spirits would come, too. But if any evil spirits appeared, they tried to make enough noise to frighten them. Birthday "spanks" were one way to drive the evil spirits away.

Most birthday cakes are round. **Did you know** that people first baked round, "moon" cakes as gifts for the moon goddess?

Other people baked tiny trinkets in birthday cakes. If you found a ring in a piece of cake, it meant you would marry. A coin was a sign that you would be rich, but a thimble meant you might be poor.

How many hidden trinkets can you find?

(Do you know how to bake a birthday cake? See page 45.)

You don't have to have a birthday to give a party!

If you're hot and bored with summer, why not give an unbirthday party?
- Invite your friends to come in bathing suits. Then hand out water balloons or squirt guns as favors.
- Turn on the lawn sprinkler and play a game of water tag. Or put a tarp or sheet of plastic on a hill and wet it with a hose for a fun slide.

- Plan a scavenger hunt. Make a list of funny things that you know your friends can find, if they use their imagination. Like a shoelace, a book, a clover leaf, a button, a hair ribbon. (Be sure to check with your family about this first, and set limits where your guests can hunt.)
- Bake an unbirthday cake.

BIRTHDAY PIÑATA

In Mexico and other Spanish-speaking countries, a popular birthday party game uses a piñata (say pin-YA-ta). A piñata is a colorful animal or shape made out of paper, and filled with candy or party favors. Each party guest is given a stick, then blindfolded. The person who breaks open the piñata is said to have good luck. Everyone gets to enjoy the goodies inside.

You need:
- Large balloon, blown up and tied
- Newspapers, cut or torn in strips about 1" wide
- Wallpaper paste
- Candies or party favors in a small bag
- Transparent tape
- 5 small paper cups
- Colored crepe paper, including pink
- White glue
- Markers
- Pipe cleaner, curled for tail
- Pink paper, cut into triangles for ears
- Twine or string

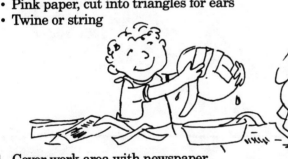

1. Cover work area with newspaper.
2. Prepare a quart of wallpaper paste according to the directions on the box.
3. From fold to edge, tear newspapers into 1" strips.
4. Pull each strip through paste.
5. Cover the whole balloon with one layer of paper. Then repeat layers until you have at least 5 covering the balloon.
6. Let paper mache dry completely.
7. Tape bag of "goodies" to belly of the "pig."
8. Attach paper cups for feet and snout with tape.
9. Wrap "pig" with pink crepe paper, and glue edges to paper mache. Leave paper loose on back for a tail.
10. Make face with markers, and write "Hit" over pig's belly. Add pipe cleaner tail (run through loose paper, before glueing). Glue on ears.
11. When it's time for your party, hang up the piñata with string. Make two loops – one behind his front legs and the other in front of his back legs.

SEPTEMBER

At one time, the calendar started in March. September was the seventh month of the year. It is named for the Latin word for "seven." (Can you write the Roman numerals for "7"?) Nowadays, the calendar starts in January, so September is the ninth month of the year.

Lots of things happen in these 30 days. School starts! Fall begins! Many birds migrate south. The days get shorter, and the air gets cooler.

Connect the dots to see who gets the ribbon.

"September blow soft
Till the fruit's in the loft."

To farmers, this means: "Let's hope it doesn't turn cold until we've picked the fruit off the trees."

September is the time to celebrate bringing in the harvest. In America, there are country fairs.

CALENDAR DATES
• LABOR DAY 1ST MONDAY
• FIRST DAY OF SCHOOL
• 21 FIRST DAY OF FALL
• GRANDPARENT'S DAY 2nd Sunday

Asters are September's special flowers. Sapphires are the lucky stone. Do you know what color they both are? Hint: If it's a clear day, look up.

FARMER BROWN'S STAND

Here is a coloring page of "Farmer Brown's Stand." Seven of his fruits
and vegetables begin with vowels. Can you find them?

In the empty boxes, draw vegetables or fruits that begin with the letters on the boxes.

How many fruits or vegetables start with these vowels?

A ___ E ___ I ___ O ___ U ___ Y ___

To help you find the fruits and vegetables, use this color code:

✝ = Yellow   ○ = Red   ∩ = Blue   ★ = Green   △ = Orange   ■ = Purple

LABOR DAY

Labor Day is the time we honor all those who work hard. This US national holiday falls on the first Monday in September. For many people, Labor Day means the end of summer—the last chance to have a picnic or cookout. For others, this holiday means school will start soon.

Look at all these different laborers. Some have misplaced an important tool of their trade. Help them on Labor Day by drawing a line to connect the workers with what they need to do their jobs. If you unscramble the names of their jobs, it might help.

R A P T C E N R E

T A U N O R T S A

S T E N N I

R O P

S U N R E

I S R T A T

C A R D E N

N E R I M

W L O N C

N I M U S A I C

L O P S T A   R K O R E W

🍎 THE FIRST DAY OF SCHOOL 🍎

No matter how old we may be, everybody remembers the first day of school! Maybe this will be your first day—at pre-school, grade school, or a new school. This is an exciting day, but it can be a little scary, too.

In Germany, children get a paper cone filled with "goodies" to help "sweeten" the day. You can make one to help someone who may be a little nervous about starting school—or to enjoy yourself. Fill the cone with candy and cookies.

You need:
- Construction paper
- Pencil
- Scissors
- Transparent tape
- Yarn and/or crepe paper
- White glue

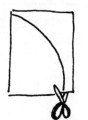

1. Cut paper into a 22" square. With a pencil, draw a curve from one corner to the next and cut out that line.
2. Roll paper, so that the two straight edges overlap an inch or so. Tape the cone together.
3. Glue on yarn or crepe paper bows to decorate.
4. Fill with "goodies."

For many American children, a _ _ _ _ _ _ _ _ _ means the start of school—and begins all the other fun days there, as well. Connect the dots to draw this American sign of school.

GRANDPARENTS' DAY

Grandparents' Day is the second Sunday in September. It is a time to be extra nice to these special people for all the things they have done for you.

What was it like when your grandparents were your age? Why don't you ask them some questions? (If you have a tape recorder, ask them if it's all right to tape their answers. Then you'll have a permanent record of their memories.) What was school like in their day? What clothes did they wear? What did they do for fun? Who were their friends? What were their parents like? Don't interrupt your grandparents. They'll answer questions you hadn't even thought to ask.

Ask your grandparents if all the things in this picture were around when they were growing up. Look carefully at this picture. Try to remember everything you see in it. Then turn to page 125 and answer the questions.

Monarch Butterfly Migration

Every September, millions of monarch (say: MON-ark) butterflies fly from their summer homes to their winter homes. They travel thousands of miles from Canada and the northern states to Mexico and Southern California.

Did you know?

These pretty, orange and black insects can fly as fast as 30 miles per hour. (How fast can you run?)

Sometimes tree branches break when too many monarchs rest in the same place.

Birds don't eat them because they taste bad.

If you would like to learn more about these pretty insects, read *The Monarch Butterfly*, by Gail Gibbons.

**HOW MANY MONARCHS CAN YOU FIND
IN THIS FIELD OF MILKWEED?**

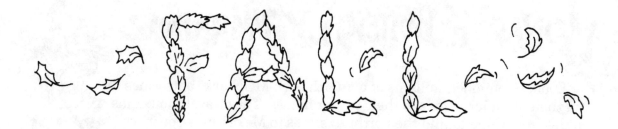

On September 23, day and night are the same length. It is the first day of fall. What's another name for this season?

N U U M T A

In the fall, leaves start to turn color. Squirrels gather nuts. Many birds migrate south. The days get colder and the nights longer. Seeds blow in the wind.

Try keeping a milkweed seed in the air without touching it.

What tree does this come from?

See if this maple seed flies like a helicopter.

Try and catch one.

Elm trees start from these little seeds!

What's the world's biggest seed? A coconut. It travels by floating on the water.

Some seeds are hitch hikers. They don't blow in the wind. Instead, they attach themselves to other things, like clothing and fur. They get a free ride.

THINGS TO MAKE WITH WALNUT SHELLS

Did you know that nuts are seeds? How many things can you make with walnut shells?

You need:
- Walnut shell halves
- Construction paper
- Pipe cleaners
- Scissors
- Glue
- Assorted marking pens
- Cotton balls
- String

Look at these pictures and create as shown.

Glue shell on cut-out shape

TURTLE

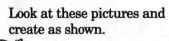

WHALE

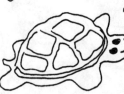

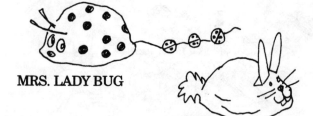

MRS. LADY BUG

RABBIT

MOUSE

Pipe cleaner

OLD LADY

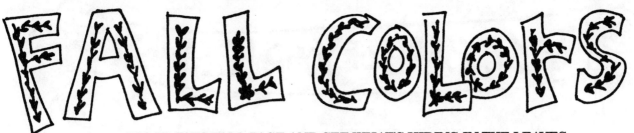

FALL COLORS

COLOR THIS FALL PAGE AND SEE WHAT'S HIDING IN THE LEAVES

• = red   •• = yellow   ••• = orange   ∴ = brown   .∷ = black

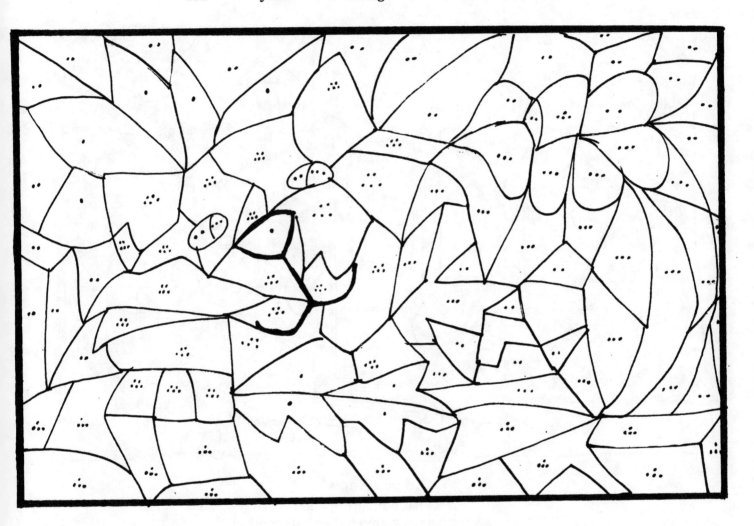

   Questions for Grandparent's Day Page. DON'T READ THIS UNTIL
YOU'VE LOOKED AT PAGE 122.

1. What time is it?
2. What is the baby wearing on its head?
3. What kind of bird is on the lawn?
4. What is the boy riding?
5. How many cars are in the picture?
6. What is the boy pushing?
7. What is the man carrying?

Now look at page 122 and see how many answers you
got right. Give this page to a grandparent to try. Is
their memory as good as yours?

TAKE CARE OF YOUR PET WEEK

"Take Care Of Your Pet Week" is always the last week in September.
Do you have a pet? What kind? How many pets can you find in this picture?

Did you know?
If a kitten hasn't opened
its eyes yet it's too young to leave its mother.
Male canaries are the best singers.
The best time to adopt a puppy is when it is 6 to 8 weeks old.

Pets deserve good care.
To learn more about how to treat your pet,
you could read a book. Some interesting ones include:

Choosing Your Pet, by Mark McPherson
A Step-by-Step Book About Canaries, by Anmarie Barrie.
Understanding Cats, by Bridget Gibbs.
Know Your Pet: Dogs, by Anna and Michael Sproule.
Making Friends with Guinea Pigs, by Lilo Hess.
Insect Pets: Catching and Caring for Them, by Carla Stevens,
illustrated by Karl W. Stuecklen.

Good Neighbor Day

Whether we live in a big city or far out in the country, we all have neighbors. Some are just closer than others! What would life be like without our neighbors? Some neighbors drop by to welcome us when we move to a new place. Others may be our first friends – or our first sitters.

In the US, the fourth Sunday in September is officially Good Neighbor Day. This is a great day to repay your neighbors for all the nice things they have done for you and your family! You might offer to bring a neighbor her mail, rake a neighbor's lawn, or make cookies for those who don't have the time or feel well enough to do these jobs themselves. Some towns ask everyone to pick up trash along the road-side on Good Neighbor Day.

Easy No-Bake Cookies

You need:
1 cup honey
1 cup peanut butter
1 cup nonfat dry milk
1 cup semi-sweet chocolate bits
1 cup graham cracker crumbs
   or rolled oats

1. Mix first four ingredients together.
2. Chill dough in refrigerator, then shape into balls when cool enough to work well (about a half hour).
3. Roll in crumbs or oats. Store in a cool place.
   Makes about 60 cookies.

How many words can you make from neighbor?

_____

_____

_____

_____

_____

_____

_____

_____

_____

_____

See Through Pictures

You need:
• Pictures that you have crayoned or cut out from old magazines
• Gel medium from an art store or craft shop.

1. Collect your favorite pictures to share.
2. Mix gel, according to instructions on the package.
3. Brush 12 coats of gel on each picture, letting each coat dry before adding a new one.
4. After the last coat dries, soak each picture in water. Then peel off the paper. Your picture will be left on the gel, and will be fun to hang in a window.

Don't you feel nice when you do something for someone else?

NATIVE AMERICAN DAY

The fourth Friday of September is a day to honor American Indians. It is called Native American Day.

Do you know who greeted the Pilgrims when they landed in Massachusetts? Indians. They had already been living in America for thousands of years. They were friendly, and helped the Pilgrims start their colony.

Did you know Native Americans taught us to grow potatoes, corn, beans, and tomatoes? They also taught us how to make popcorn, roast peanuts, and even chew gum.

When the Pilgrims landed, about one million Native Americans lived in North America. Today, about one and a half million live in the US. Do you know which state has the most Native Americans? California.

WAMPUM NECKLACE

Long ago, Indians didn't carry wallets. They wore money around their necks. Their money was shells and beads. It was called "wampum."

You can make a wampum necklace. All you need are colored straws and string.

1. Cut the string so it is long enough to go comfortably around your head when it's tied together.
2. Cut straws into 1" pieces.
3. Thread pieces onto string, alternating colors. (Put a book on the other end of string, so wampum doesn't fall off as you work.)
4. When the string is full, tie the ends together.
5. To look like you are a wealthy Indian, make several necklaces and wear them all at the same time.

INDIAN NAMES

There are many Indian names in North America: Chicago, Mississippi, Ottowa, Delaware, Omaha, Miami. Can you think of others?
Native Americans also gave us many of the words we use today. There are sixteen Indian words in this puzzle. Try to find them all. Look up, down, sideways, backwards, and diagonally.

Persimmon
Powwow
Raccoon
Squash
Succotash
Toboggan
Tomahawk
Wigwam

Coyote
Eskimo
Kayak
Moccasin
Moose
Opossum
Papoose
Pecan

```
R Y N F R J T K I X L N
A E W L O P O S S U M P
C B T I H O E F Q A O E
C X N U G W D C U Y K R
O R I L T W O H A B O S
O E S E N O A B S N R I
N C A V T W B M H C D M
I H C P A P O O S E K M
E Q C E S O O M G U R O
Z C O Y O T E I B G C N
T O M A H A W K A Y A K
S U C C O T A S H R X N
H Y I V M O S E N B T F
```

The Pueblo Indians of the southwestern United States wore kachina masks in ceremonies. To these Native Americans, a kachina was a spirit which could communicate with the gods. They could bring rain or make crops grow. The Pueblos painted colors and designs on the masks. Each design was a symbol.

To make a blank mask, draw a rectangle on a large sheet of paper. Add small shapes for the eyes and mouth. Then decorate with some of the symbols shown here. After the mask is all decorated, you can color it.

The Pueblos liked yellow, blue-green, red, white, and black.

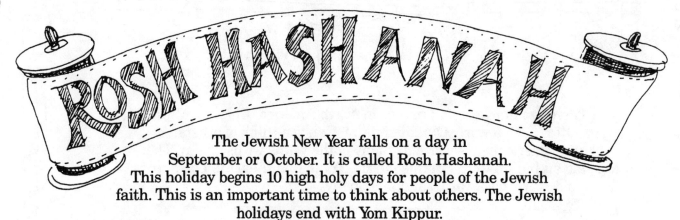

ROSH HASHANAH

The Jewish New Year falls on a day in September or October. It is called Rosh Hashanah. This holiday begins 10 high holy days for people of the Jewish faith. This is an important time to think about others. The Jewish holidays end with Yom Kippur.

At Rosh Hashanah, Jewish people send cards to family and friends. They wish each other *"Shanan Tobah,"* or "a good year." And they eat sweet foods, so the new year will be sweet, too.

Jewish people go to temple and hear the *shofar*, a curved ram's horn. If you connect the dots, you can draw a *shofar*. T'KEEah! T'KEEah! T'KEEah! goes this horn.

MAKE A ROSH HASHANAH SWEET

To make a Rosh Hashanah sweet, try apple slices dipped in honey. This is an easy dish to make. Ask a grown-up to help you, if you use a knife:

You need:
• 2 apples, washed
• paring knife and/or apple corer
• honey

1. Core one end of an apple and hollow out the inside. (Use this apple as a cup to hold the honey.)
2. Slice the other apple and arrange slices on a plate around the apple "cup."
3. Fill the "cup" with honey. Dip slices in honey and enjoy!

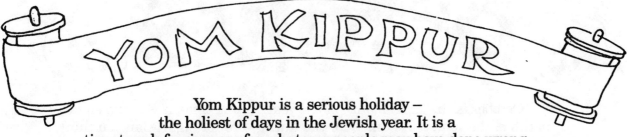

YOM KIPPUR

Yom Kippur is a serious holiday –
the holiest of days in the Jewish year. It is a
time to ask forgiveness for whatever people may have done wrong.
On Yom Kippur, Jewish people often give food or money to those in need.
Some go all day without eating – they fast. Many people wear white, as a
sign of hope and purity, when they go to temple. There they hear the story
of Jonah read aloud.
Jonah did not do what God asked. Instead, he sailed away. But God sent a
storm, and Jonah was tossed overboard. Then he was swallowed by a
whale. When he prayed to God for forgiveness, the whale spit him out on
dry land. God gave Jonah another chance to do his duty. Like Jonah, all
Jews promise God they will do better, if He will forgive them.
When the *shofar* sounds once more, the Yom Kippur fast is over.

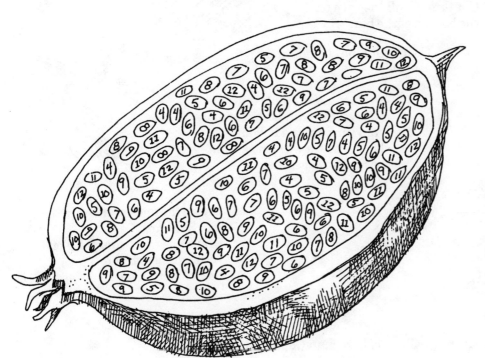

Do you know why Jews cut
pomegranates open during the
high holidays? The pomegranate
is full of seeds. It is said the
number of seeds equals the
number of good deeds Jewish
people do for others.

How many good deeds did
you do this year? Color all the
seeds with your age on them.
Then count them up.

To get through their fast on Yom Kippur, some Jewish
people find it helps to smell something good – like this
spicy apple.

You need:
• Fresh apple
• Lots of cloves
• Ribbon

1. Stick cloves in the apple until it has a strong, pungent scent.
2. Tie a ribbon around the apple, or onto its stem.

OCTOBER

October is the ___th month of the year. At one time, it was the eighth month of the year. It is named for the Latin word for eight. Can you think of anything else that begins with "octo"?

If you were born this month, the dahlia is your flower, and your lucky stone is the opal.

MAKE AN OCTOPUS

1. Wrap the whole skein around the long side of cereal box.
2. Cut through all the yarn on the bottom of the box.

3. Count out nine strands and set aside.

You need:
- Skein of yarn
- Scissors
- Cereal box
- 3" styrofoam ball
- 2 black buttons
- Needle and thread

4. Divide the rest evenly and make an "X" with both clumps.
5. Wrap yarn around ball as shown and tie with one strand that you saved earlier.

6. Divide the ends of the yarn into 8 clumps.
7. Braid legs and tie each leg off with another strand.
8. Sew on button eyes.

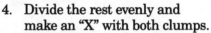

Do you remember reading about the swallows of San Juan Capistrano? They almost always arrive at the mission on the same day in March. Well, they also usually leave on the same day every October! The 23rd.

In Bolivia, a country in South America, there is a fair in October, called Alacitas (say: All-a-SEE-tas). At the fair, people can buy things in miniature size —tiny chairs, tables, dolls, sacks of flour, cans of gasoline, even houses. Fairgoers can also buy a tiny clay man. They hang the miniature things they bought on his back. People think the clay man is magical. They hope he will bring them all the things he carries during the coming year.

CALENDAR DATES

COLUMBUS DAY celebrated the 2nd Monday (Traditionally Oct. 12)

HALLOWEEN - 31

OCTOBER GATHERING

"Fresh October brings the pheasant;
Then to gather nuts is pleasant."

October is when squirrels gather acorns and hide them. What kind of tree
do acorns come from?

If Mrs. Squirrel hides an acorn every day in October except four, how many
will she have to eat during the winter? If you find all the acorns hidden in
this picture, you will have the correct answer.

COLUMBUS DAY

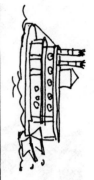

"Fourteen Hundred and Ninety Two,
Columbus Sailed the Ocean Blue."

October 12 is the day Christopher Columbus discovered America in 1492. People in the US celebrate this national holiday on the second Monday in October. Hawaiians not only honor Columbus on this day, but also the sailors from Polynesia who discovered their islands in the Pacific Ocean.

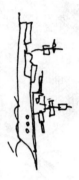

Columbus and 89 sailors sailed from Spain on three ships: the *Nina,* the *Pinta,* and the *Santa Maria.* They were hoping to find a new route to Japan and China.

When they landed on San Salvador, an island in the Bahamas, Columbus knew it wasn't Japan or China, but he didn't realize he had landed on a whole new continent. You could say that America was discovered by mistake!

Did you know?

- Another man actually discovered America almost 500 years before Columbus. His name was Leif Erikson. While on a voyage to Greenland from his home in Iceland, he was blown off course and landed somewhere in Canada.

- Columbus brought lots of cats with him on his voyage to America. The cats were supposed to eat the rats on board.

- Columbus and his men sailed from Spain to America in 37 days. How long do you think it would take to fly?

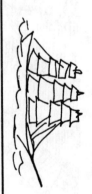

Can you find the *Santa Maria* among these crafts?

Make the *Nina, Pinta,* and *Santa Maria* as shown below:

HALF WALNUT SHELL

MODELING CLAY

TOOTHPICK

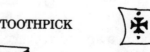
PAPER SAIL

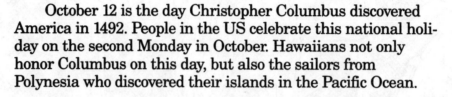

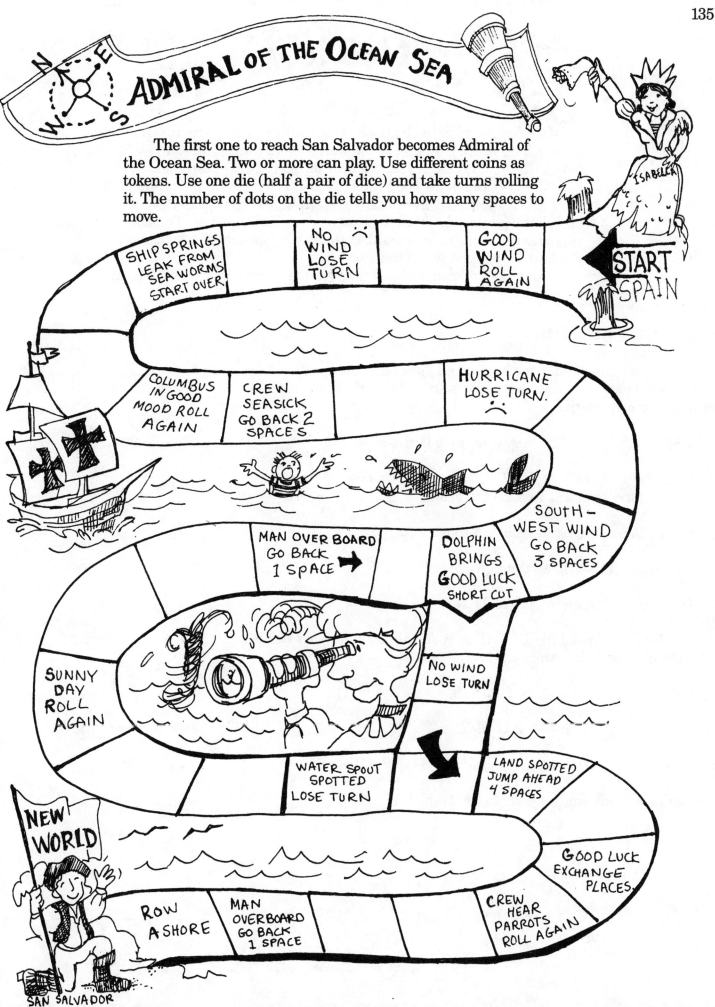

ADMIRAL OF THE OCEAN SEA

The first one to reach San Salvador becomes Admiral of the Ocean Sea. Two or more can play. Use different coins as tokens. Use one die (half a pair of dice) and take turns rolling it. The number of dots on the die tells you how many spaces to move.

START SPAIN

ISABELLA

SHIP SPRINGS LEAK FROM SEA WORMS START OVER

NO WIND LOSE TURN

GOOD WIND ROLL AGAIN

COLUMBUS IN GOOD MOOD ROLL AGAIN

CREW SEASICK GO BACK 2 SPACES

HURRICANE LOSE TURN.

MAN OVER BOARD GO BACK 1 SPACE

DOLPHIN BRINGS GOOD LUCK SHORT CUT

SOUTH-WEST WIND GO BACK 3 SPACES

SUNNY DAY ROLL AGAIN

NO WIND LOSE TURN

WATER SPOUT SPOTTED LOSE TURN

LAND SPOTTED JUMP AHEAD 4 SPACES

GOOD LUCK EXCHANGE PLACES.

NEW WORLD

ROW ASHORE

MAN OVERBOARD GO BACK 1 SPACE

CREW HEAR PARROTS ROLL AGAIN

SAN SALVADOR

UNITED NATIONS DAY

October 24 is United Nations Day. It celebrates an organization that tries to keep peace throughout the world. More than 155 countries belong to the UN, as it is called. It is our only form of world government.

The UN does many good things. It sends experts to poor countries to teach them about modern medicine, teaching, and farming. It sends food and clothing to needy children in more than 100 countries. The UN encourages artists to paint, scientists to invent, teachers to teach, and thinkers to think. It fights hunger.

But most important, the United Nations works hard to keep countries from fighting each other.

P A A N J

NAME THAT COUNTRY

See if you can unscramble the letters and guess the countries in these sentences. Then try to find them on a map of the world in an atlas, almanac or dictionary.

1. The S R S U is the largest country in the world.

2. H E T D E U I N T T T S S E A was the first country to land a man on the moon.

3. U T I A A S R A L is also a continent.

4. The Amazon river flows through Z L B A I R.

5. Divali is celebrated in I I A D N.

6. Leif Erikson landed in D N C A A A   almost 500 years before Columbus sailed to America.

7. Columbus sailed from N I A P S.

8. The pyramids are in P T G E Y.

9. P A A N J is made up of many islands in the Pacific Ocean.

10. Animals represent the years in A H N I C.

P T G E

A H N I C

N I A P S

I I A D N

Z L B A I R

D N C A A A

S R S U

U T I A A S R A L

H T E D E U I N T T T S S E A

"WORLD WEAR"

The boy in this picture has borrowed clothes from friends who live in other parts of the world. Can you draw a line from the article of clothing to the friend who lent it to him? What's in his hand? Who does it belong to?

ARGENTINA

AUSTRALIA

HOLLAND

SCOTLAND

AFRICA

SWITZERLAND

ALASKA

RUSSIA

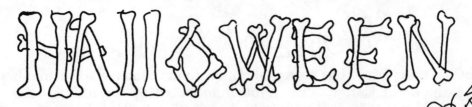

HALLOWEEN

The last day of October is the ___st. You know what happens on that night? Goblins and witches and ghosts and demons and all other kinds of scary things come out of their hiding places to haunt us. It's Halloween! But you know, those scary things don't really exist—or do they? Of course not, but kids still dress up in costumes to frighten them away—*just in case!*

Halloween began with the Celts—people who lived in France and the British Isles long ago. The Celts worshipped the sun, and did not like darkness. They especially disliked winter, when it got dark early. The Celts thought evil spirits made the sun disappear earlier each day. So they built a huge bonfire on the night we call Halloween to frighten the evil spirits away.

When you go trick-or-treating on Halloween, here are some rules to follow:

- Carry a flashlight if it's very dark. Hold it under your chin to spook people. And, of course, it helps you see where you're going and what monsters are heading your way.

- Don't take treats from people you don't know.

- If you are seven years old or younger, go trick-or-treating with a parent before it gets dark. Go only to homes where you know the people.

- Don't eat any treats until you get home. Check them over with a parent, and throw out any that don't seem ok. Don't eat your "loot" all at once. Put some in a jar and see how long you can make it last.

- If you are eight or older, do your trick-or-treating between 6:30 and 7:30. Go with a group of friends, and don't get separated. Stay in the neighborhood, and go only to houses where you know the people.

SKULL PUPPET

You need:
- White construction paper (2 sheets 9" x 12")
- Markers
- Scissors
- Tape or glue

1. Fold long side of one piece of paper in thirds.

2. Tape to hold shut.

3. Fold in half. Fold each open end out to look like "M".

4. Insert fingers in one opening and thumb in other. (Note mouth movement.)

5. Draw skull on ½ sheet of paper (6" x 9")

6. Glue or tape skull "head" to top fold and jaw to bottom.

Jaw

(Add [anything "gross" to your skull.])

Did you know Halloween is a national holiday in Ireland?

November

The eleventh month of the year is November. At one time it was the ninth month, so is named for the Latin word for nine.

In northern countries, November can be cold and gray. The days are short and the nights are long. This can be a dreary time of year. But people have ways of brightening things up.

In the US, we celebrate with our national harvest festival: Thanksgiving.

In Japan, they have the "Seven-Five-Three Festival." It's a special time for children who are seven, five, or three years old. In the box below are presents for each child. What presents go to which children?

"Dull November brings the blast;
Then the leaves are whirling fast."

If you have a birthday in November, your special flower is the chrysthanthemum, and your lucky stone is the topaz.

CALENDAR DATES
ELECTION DAY - 1ST TUES. FOLLOWING a MONDAY
VETERANS' DAY 11
THANKSGIVING (4TH THURSDAY)

WINTER SLEEPERS

"Dull November brings the blast;
Then the leaves are whirling fast."

In November, before the snow flakes fly, many animals escape the cold by going to sleep. Some animals—like bears, chipmunks, skunks, and raccoons—just snooze. They wake up on warm days. They stretch their legs and grab a bite to eat—if they can find something. Other animals stay asleep all winter long. They are called hibernators. Woodchucks, bats, wasps, and spiders are hibernators.

Where do all these animals sleep? Woodchucks and chipmunks sleep in underground dens. Bears and bats sleep in caves. Bats hang upside down from the ceiling. Frogs and some fishes bury themselves in mud at the bottom of ponds. Turtles dig holes in the ground. Snakes slither into crevices between rocks or trees. Wasps, spiders, and ladybugs crawl under rocks and logs or dig under the bark of trees.

Can you copy these sleepy animals and put them in their beds?

Divali India's Festival of Lights

The people of India believe that Lakshmi, the goddess of luck and wealth, lives with the stars in the sky. To lure her to earth, they choose one day each year to make the world look as bright and beautiful as the heavens. This holiday is known as Divali.

On a dark moonless night in November, Indians decorate their homes and yards with as many tiny lamps as they can afford to light. Today, they use candles and electric lights, too.

The whole country celebrates this festival of lights. People clean their homes. After the long rainy season, "fall" housecleaning is a happy time. Once everything and everyone is clean, children put lamps everywhere. At sunset, people say their prayers, and parents tell their children the story of Lakshmi, the goddess of luck and wealth. As soon as it is dark, people light all their lamps. Every home, street, town and city glitter and shine. India looks like the starry sky.

Make a Divali Lamp

You need:
• self-hardening clay
• pencil
• wicks
• vegetable oil

1. Make a 2 1/2-inch clay ball with your hands.

2. Press this ball on a flat surface to make a disc about 1 1/4 inches thick.

3. Turn your disc, smoothing the edges with your fingers and pressing your thumbs into the center to make a flat bowl.

4. Make a lip to hold the wick, by pulling clay out one side, pressing with a pencil.
5. Using the pencil point, cut a design on your lamp.
6. Let clay dry, according to instructions on the package.

7. Coil wick in bowl and pull one end out the lip. It should extend a half inch past the lip to light easily.
8. Cover wick coil with oil and ask a grown-up if you may light it.

Read the story on the next page. (Or ask someone to read it to you.) Then help the poor washerwoman find the Queen's pearls. (Color the sandy ground yellow, but leave the pearls white.)

Lakshmi and the Wise Washer Woman

One Divali, a rich Queen went to the river to bathe for the holiday. She wore a new gift from her husband—a beautiful necklace of rare and perfect pearls. Before she dove into the water, she gave her necklace to her servants to guard. Suddenly, a crow flew down and snatched the precious necklace. The servants screamed and chased the bird. But the crow was too quick for them.

The Queen was very upset. Back at the palace, she wept before the King because her necklace was lost. He ordered messengers to run far and wide offering a reward for the Queen's pearls. But the crow flew farther away than even the King's messengers could go. Finally, the bird stopped to rest outside a poor washerwoman's hut. Finding that pearls tasted terrible, the crow dropped the necklace and flew off in search of something better to eat.

When the hard-working washerwoman returned home, she saw the beautiful necklace lying in the dirt. The woman had heard the King's message and knew she was in luck! Quickly she rushed to the Palace, carrying the Queen's necklace. The King offered her a purse full of money, but the washerwoman refused it. Since this was Divali, she had another reward in mind.

"I do not want money," she told the King.

"But this would keep you well-fed and handsomely-clothed for years," the King reasoned.

"I ask one wish, instead," she said. And the King promised to grant it, whatever it might be.

"Light no lamps, tonight," the washer-woman asked. "And allow no one but me to light a lamp." Thinking he had gotten off easily, the King happily granted her wish. No one lighted any lamps, except the poor washerwoman.

As usual, Lakshmi left the heavens and ventured down to earth. But instead of seeing hundreds of thousands of twinkling lights, the world was filled with darkness. Poor Lakshmi stumbled along, unable to see where she was going. Then, she saw a glimmer of light. She ran towards it. A tired, sad Lakshmi came upon the poor washerwoman's hut. "Let me in," she cried, banging loudly on the door.

"Only if you promise you will stay with me for seven generations," answered the wise washerwoman.

"Let me in," Lakshmi begged, crying and hating the dark. "I will do anything you ask." The washerwoman opened her door and was blessed with good fortune for as long as she and her family lived. Even today, her descendants may enjoy good luck, as long as they continue to welcome Lakshmi.

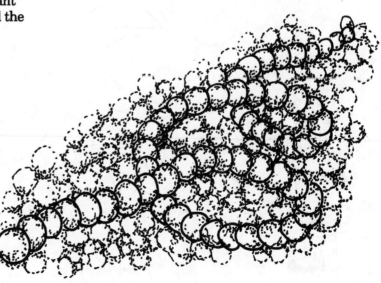

Brother and Sister Day

In India, Hindu sisters and brothers have a special day to show their friendship toward each other. On November 3, a sister puts red makeup on her forehead. Next, she draws a round design of the universe on the floor with rice powder. The design is called a mandala. Then she asks her brother to sit in the middle of the mandala while she wishes him happiness.

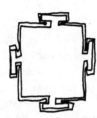  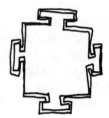

This is a mandala design. Try creating your own.

Hindu sisters sometimes tie colored scarves on their brothers' wrists to show their friendship. The brothers promise to take care of their sisters and give them jewelry, clothing, or money.

These sisters and brothers have gotten their scarves tangled. Color the scarves to find out who are related to each other.

R = Red   O = Orange   Y = Yellow

☆ELECTION DAY☆

Election Day is an important holiday in a democracy like the US. Any citizen over 18 years old gets to vote for the people who govern each state—and sometimes our whole country! Presidential elections come every four years, but state elections are held more often. So are city or county elections.

Election Day is always the Tuesday that follows the first Monday in November. If people want any say in their government, it is important that they learn something about the candidates running for office. And that they vote on Election Day!

You don't have to be 18 to practice voting. Some schools hold "mock" elections and give all the students a chance to vote on Election Day. Or you can choose one of the "candidates" in this picture.

In the US, most people belong to one of two political parties. The donkey represents the Democratic Party. The Republican Party uses the elephant as its symbol. There are always some independent candidates, who do not belong to one of the major parties. Independents can't agree on one symbol, because they have so many different ideas.

Take a poll of the animals in this picture. How many donkeys, elephants, and other animals are there? Using the bar graph below, show which party is ahead in the presidential election. (Hint: Sometimes independents will vote for a candidate from one of the major parties. Look carefully before you make your graph.)

The Republican candidate is Mr. Smith. The Democratic candidate is Mrs. Jones.

									DEMOCRATS
									REPUBLICANS

Color a box blue for each vote for a Democratic candidate.
Color a box red for each vote for a Republican candidate.

VETERANS' DAY

November 11 celebrates the armistice, or peace, that ended World War I. People thought there would be no more war. But they were wrong.

In countries like Canada, England, France, and the US, people honor those who died in both World Wars on Armistice Day. Americans changed the name of the holiday to Veterans' Day. That way we can remember all those who served in the armed forces during all the wars our country has fought.

Can you identify each armed service by its uniform? Match the number for each branch of military service with the pictures below.

R A I L O S

I protect
our seas.

D O L I E R S

My most important
job is national defense.

R A M I N E

I guard our
embassies abroad.

L I P O T

My branch of the armed
services is the newest.

S O A T C

M A G U A D R N S

I help boaters and work to
keep drugs out of our country.

Navy 1   Army 2   Marines 3   Air Force 4   Coast Guard 5

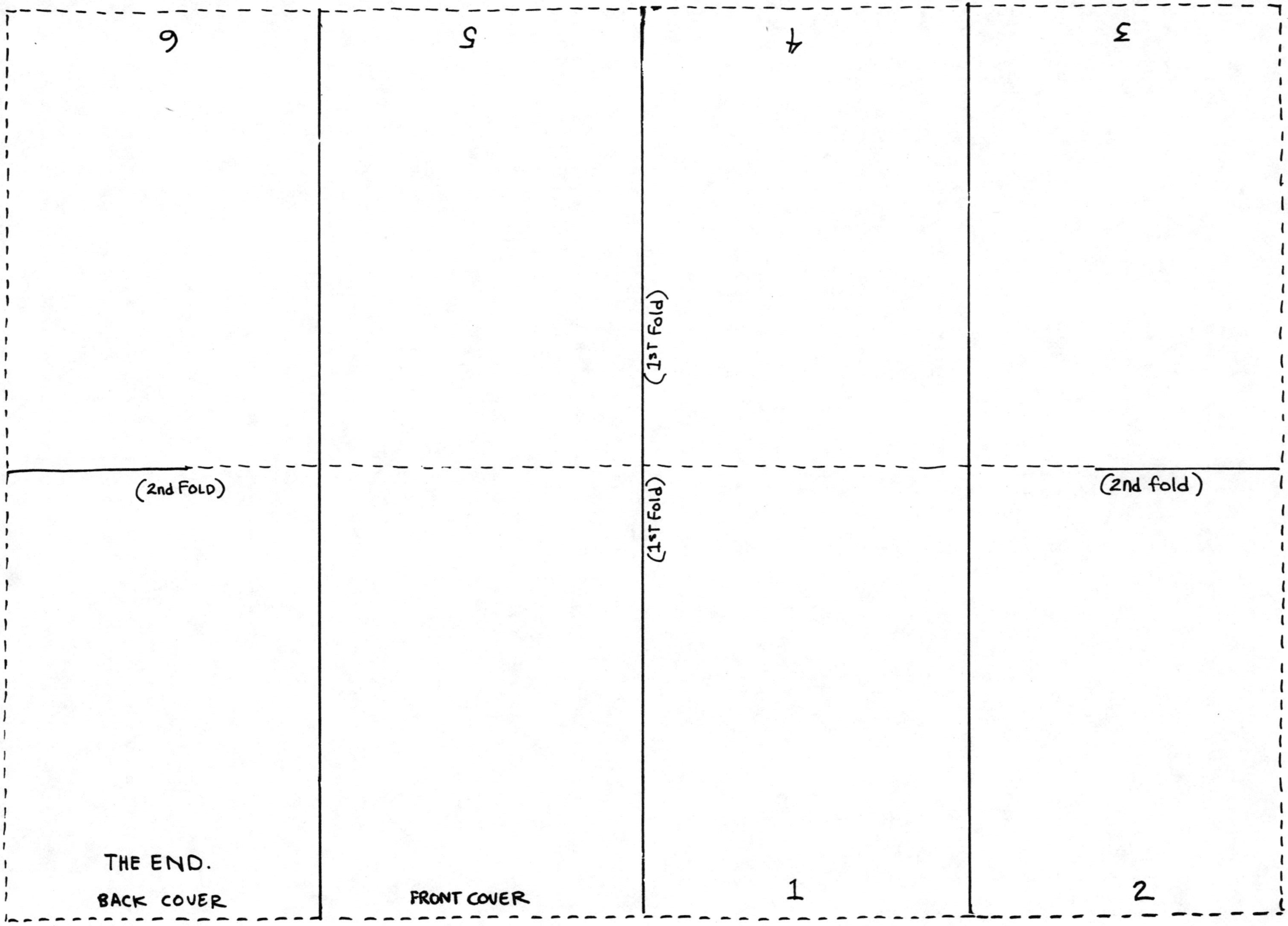

9

THE END.
BACK COVER

(2nd Fold)

5

FRONT COVER

(1st Fold) (1st Fold)

1

4

2

(2nd fold)

3

CHILDREN'S BOOK WEEK

The third full week in November is always Children's Book Week. During this week, libraries and schools have a lot of interesting programs. You might join a contest to see how many books you can read that week – or listen to a famous children's author read your favorite book. Who is your favorite author?

Did you know?

Theodor (Dr. Seuss) Giesel worked as a cartoonist and Hollywood animator before he began to write children's books.

Maurice Sendak was a sickly boy, who loved stories like *Pinocchio* and *The Phantom of the Opera,* but hated school.

Madeleine L'Engle has written stories ever since she was old enough to hold a pencil. If she has something to say that is too difficult for adults to swallow, then she puts it in a book for kids.

Can you write each author's name after the books she or he wrote?

Meet the Austins _____

Green Eggs and Ham _____

Chicken Soup with Rice _____

Where the Wild Things Are _____

A Wrinkle in Time _____

The Sneeches _____

(If you haven't already read these books, Children's Book Week is a good time to start.)

When you grow up, you might want to be a children's author or illustrator. You can create your first book by coloring and assembling pages 147-8.

Make your Own Book!

1. Cut along the dotted lines.

2. Fold at the first fold line.

3. Open. Fold at the second fold line.

4. Holding each end, push inward.

5. Pinch the pages together, so front and back covers enclose them.

6. Crease the edge where the pages come together (people call this the spine of a book). Fill in the blanks on each page with "your story" and color "your illustrations." Have fun!

THANKSGIVING

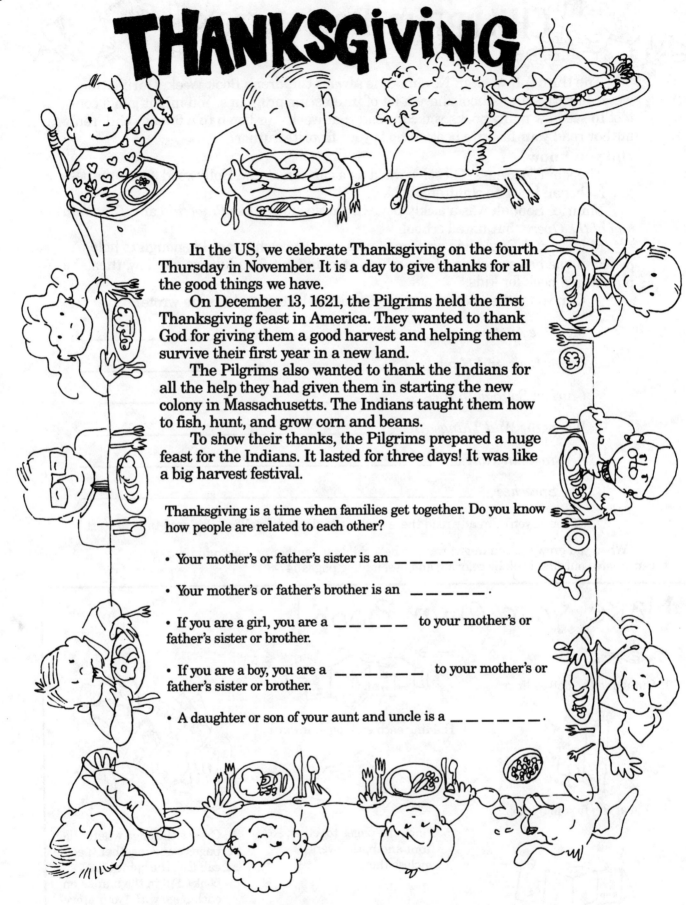

In the US, we celebrate Thanksgiving on the fourth Thursday in November. It is a day to give thanks for all the good things we have.

On December 13, 1621, the Pilgrims held the first Thanksgiving feast in America. They wanted to thank God for giving them a good harvest and helping them survive their first year in a new land.

The Pilgrims also wanted to thank the Indians for all the help they had given them in starting the new colony in Massachusetts. The Indians taught them how to fish, hunt, and grow corn and beans.

To show their thanks, the Pilgrims prepared a huge feast for the Indians. It lasted for three days! It was like a big harvest festival.

Thanksgiving is a time when families get together. Do you know how people are related to each other?

• Your mother's or father's sister is an _ _ _ _ _ .

• Your mother's or father's brother is an _ _ _ _ _ _ .

• If you are a girl, you are a _ _ _ _ _ _ to your mother's or father's sister or brother.

• If you are a boy, you are a _ _ _ _ _ _ _ to your mother's or father's sister or brother.

• A daughter or son of your aunt and uncle is a _ _ _ _ _ _ _ .

"Over the river and through the woods,
to Grandmother's house we go!"

Giving thanks

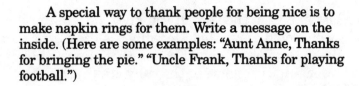

A special way to thank people for being nice is to make napkin rings for them. Write a message on the inside. (Here are some examples: "Aunt Anne, Thanks for bringing the pie." "Uncle Frank, Thanks for playing football.")

THANK YOU NAPKIN RINGS

You need:
- White or colored construction paper
- Scissors
- Colored marking pens

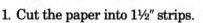

1. Cut the paper into 1½" strips.
2. Roll up a cloth napkin that will be used at Thanksgiving.
3. Wrap a paper strip one time around the napkin.
4. Cut the strip 1" longer than it takes to go around the napkin.
5. Using the first strip as a guide, cut as many strips as you need for all the napkins.
6. Cut short slits ½" from the ends of each strip. (Cut a slit on the top of one end, and the bottom on the other.)
7. Print the name of each person on one side, and a nice message on the other.
8. Make the strips into rings and connect the ends into the slits.

WHAT AM I?

I have a snood.

I have a wattle that can switch from red to white.

My head can turn different shades of blue.

I have a beard.

I'm a _ _ _ _ _ _
   Y E T U K R

A snood is the flap of skin that hangs down from the beak. A wattle is the bumpy skin on the neck.

DECEMBER

December is the last month of the year. If you know how many months there are in a year, you'll know that December is the ___th month. Christmas, Hanukkah, and New Year's Eve are this month's holidays. Holly is December's flower, and turquoise or the ruby are this month's stones. What color are they?

Winter begins on December 21 in the Northern Hemisphere. It is the shortest day of the year. What season begins in the Southern Hemisphere on the same day? Is it a short or long day in Australia?

"Chill December brings the sleet,
Blazing fire, and Christmas treat."

CALENDAR DATES

ST. LUCIA's DAY - 13
FIRST DAY OF WINTER - 21
CHRISTMAS DAY - 25
NEW YEAR'S EVE - 31

Many people have Advent calendars in December to help them wait for Christmas. The calendars have little numbered doors covering each day from December 1 to Christmas Eve. Each day, they open a new door. Behind the door is a special picture about Christmas.

ADVENT CALENDAR

You can make an Advent jigsaw puzzle. Give it to someone you like on December 1. They will have 24 little presents to open every day until Christmas.

To make an Advent jigsaw puzzle, you need:

- Sheet of paper at least 9" x 9"
- 24 matchboxes
- Pencil
- Markers
- 24 little surprises

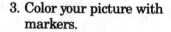

1. Measure a matchbox and sketch out 24 rectangles the same size on the sheet of paper.

2. Draw a Christmas picture.

3. Color your picture with markers.

4. Cut the picture into 24 rectangles to fit on the matchboxes.

5. Glue the rectangles onto the matchboxes.

6. Write a number from 1 to 24 in the corner of each box.

7. Put a little surprise in each matchbox: candy, little pictures, coins, jewelry, or whatever you can find that's tiny.

SANTA ANTICS

In Iceland, they have thirteen Santas. Starting on December 12th, the first Santa appears. Each day thereafter a new one shows up, until on Christmas Day all thirteen "Christmas Men" have arrived. No one ever sees these mischievous creatures, but Icelanders know they've been around. They leave gifts and other clues of their visits. One slams doors, another steals candles. A Santa might even run away with Christmas dinner!

Can you find at least thirteen differences in these pictures?   Put an X on all the ones you find.

Many Jewish holidays are celebrated in the synagogue, but the 2,000 year-old holiday, Hanukkah, is celebrated mostly at home.

Long ago, Alexander the Great conquered the known world. If you look at a map or globe, you can see that the known world then included all the lands between Greece and India. Judea, the ancient name for Israel, became part of the Greek World.

Jews there were accustomed to foreign rulers. A fair ruler, Alexander protected religious freedom. But after he died, trouble started. The new king expected everyone to worship Greek gods. He placed a statue of Zeus in the Hebrew Temple. When the Jews refused to bow down to this "graven image," soldiers burned the Temple and killed many Jews.

Under the leadership of Judah, the Hebrews fought back. At last, they won Jerusalem back from the Greeks. "Come, let us clean the Temple and make it pure again," Judah said. Children pulled up weeds that had been allowed to grow in this sacred place. Men removed the Greek statues, while women cleaned. One woman discovered a little holy oil. It still bore the seal of the priests, and the Hebrews rejoiced.

They filled the menorah, the traditional lamp. Even though there was only enough oil for one day, the menorah burned for eight days. People took this as a sign from God. Judah rededicated the temple, and the first Hanukkah was celebrated. The world *Hanukkah* means "dedication," and the holiday lasts eight days—just like the sacred oil.

Today, the Jewish people light the menorah at sundown, the beginning of the new day. Each night, another candle is lighted. An extra candle, or *shammash,* is used to light all the Hanukkah candles, and it stays lighted every night of this holiday. Can you tell what night of Hanukkah it is by looking at the pictures? (Hint: Don't forget that the shammash is lighted every night!)

MAKE A SIMPLE MENORAH

You can make your own menorah easily at home. All you need is two baking potatoes; a sharp, small knife (with a grown-up's help) and nine birthday candles. Cut bottom of potatoes, so they will lie flat, then cut four small holes in one and five small holes in the other.

Spin the Dreidel

In some families, each child has her or his own menorah. And children may receive a different small gift each day. One common Hanukkah present is a top, called dreidel (say *DRAYdull*).

Before the Hanukkah victory, Jews were not allowed to study Hebrew or worship their God. Children would study in secret. But they kept tops nearby. That way, if anyone tried to catch them studying, they could hide their books and pretend they were simply playing a game.

Dreidel is a fun game to play. You can buy dreidels that look a lot like the tops used thousands of years ago. But it's easy to make one, too!

You need:
• Cardboard (a shoe box or empty cereal box works well)
• Ruler
• Pencil
• Scissors
• Dry beans, nuts or raisins for a "kitty"

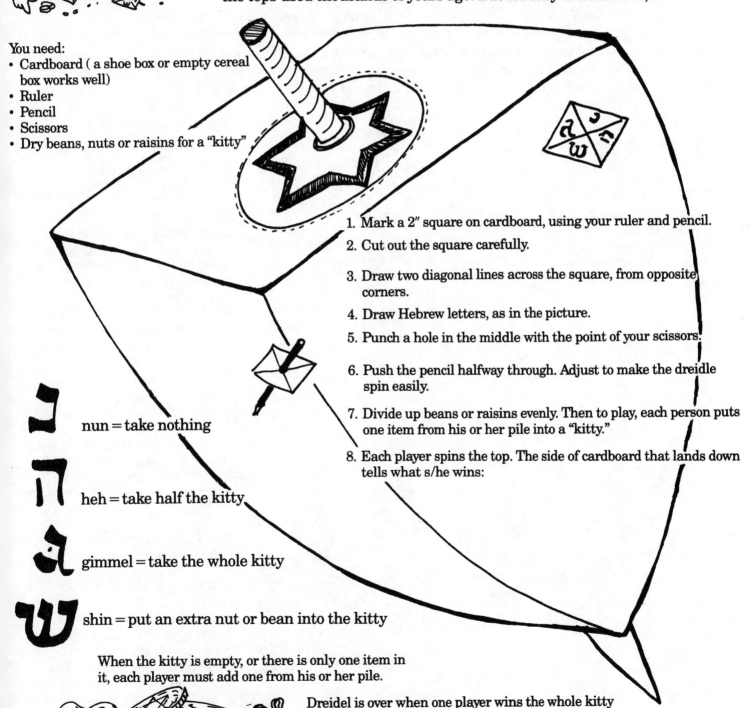

1. Mark a 2″ square on cardboard, using your ruler and pencil.

2. Cut out the square carefully.

3. Draw two diagonal lines across the square, from opposite corners.

4. Draw Hebrew letters, as in the picture.

5. Punch a hole in the middle with the point of your scissors.

6. Push the pencil halfway through. Adjust to make the dreidle spin easily.

7. Divide up beans or raisins evenly. Then to play, each person puts one item from his or her pile into a "kitty."

8. Each player spins the top. The side of cardboard that lands down tells what s/he wins:

נ nun = take nothing

ה heh = take half the kitty

ג gimmel = take the whole kitty

ש shin = put an extra nut or bean into the kitty

When the kitty is empty, or there is only one item in it, each player must add one from his or her pile.

Dreidel is over when one player wins the whole kitty and the other players have nothing left.

St. Lucia's Day

December 13 is St. Lucia's Day in Italy and Sweden. Nobody knows why an Italian saint is so popular in Scandinavia, but everyone likes this holiday. It used to be on the shortest day of the year. People celebrated the days growing longer with a Festival of Light. (What other Festivals of Light can you read about in this book?)

In Sweden, the oldest girl in the family dresses up as St. Lucia on December 13. She makes breakfast, usually saffron (or golden) buns. Then she parades through the house, serving everyone.

Each town also chooses one girl, the Lucia Queen, to lead a parade of light through the winter night. The Queen often rides on horseback. Other girls and boys follow her, singing Christmas carols. Girls wear crowns of greens with stars on them. Boys wear tall pointed caps decorated with stars. All the children dress in white clothes with red sashes, and they carry candles.

To Make Hats & Crowns

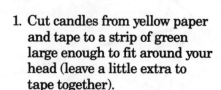

You need:
- Construction paper (yellow and green)
- Markers
- Scissors
- Transparent tape and/or a stapler

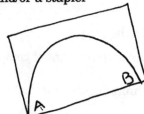

1. Cut a half circle as large as yellow paper allows.
2. Decorate semicircle with orange or red stars.
3. Match "A" and "B" corners to create a pointed hat.
4. Tape to fit your head.

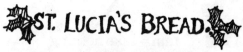

1. Cut candles from yellow paper and tape to a strip of green large enough to fit around your head (leave a little extra to tape together).
2. Cut out holly from green paper and tape on band. (Or staple real winter greens onto your crown.)

ST. LUCIA'S BREAD

If you would like to make Star Buns, the recipe is on page 159. But for an easy version of St. Lucia's bread, here's a quick recipe to try:

- Cottage cheese
- Yellow food coloring
- Cinnamon sugar, to taste
- Whole-grain bread

Mix cottage cheese with food coloring, until it looks as yellow as a candle's glow. Add a little cinnamon sugar to taste. Then spread the mixture on bread, and toast in an oven. Tastes good with hot chocolate!

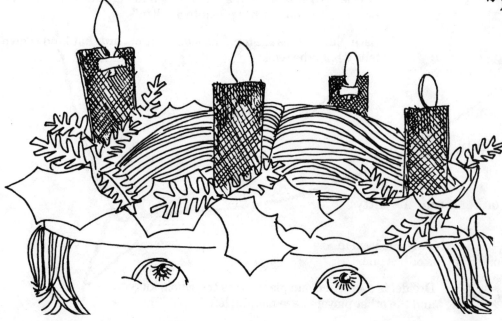

STAR OF THE DAY

Practice these dot-to-dots until you can draw stars all by yourself.

How many stars can you find in these pictures?

Which comes first? Color the pictures, then write a number to show the order of events.

Holiday Gifts to make

Whether you celebrate Christmas or Hanukkah, December is a good month to make presents for others. It's fun to have something interesting to do indoors, when it is cold outdoors and gets dark early.

Gift Bags

It's hard to have enough wrapping paper this time of year. Decorated bags make it easy to wrap any gift, no matter what its size or shape.

You need:
- Brown lunch bags
- Brown grocery bags
- Colored markers
- Newspaper
- White glue
- Colored glitter

Draw five- or six-pointed stars (depending upon which holiday *you* celebrate this month) and other holiday shapes and pictures on the bags. Or cover the floor with newspaper, and decorate bags with glue and glitter.

Did you know the custom of wrapping gifts at holiday time started in Denmark? The Danes wrap things so well that no one can guess what's inside. No fair pinching the packages to peek! Try wrapping something very small in a great big box, or a book so it looks and feels round.

Holiday Tree Ornaments

You need:
- Paper and pencil
- Leftover aluminum pans from pastry or TV dinners
- Magazines or hard rubber bath mat
- Knitting needle
- Scissors
- Markers
- Shellac or clear nail polish
- Yarn

1. Draw holiday shapes on paper and cut out.
2. Put aluminum on magazines or bath mat. Lay paper shapes on top and trace around your patterns with a pencil.
3. Remove paper and cut out aluminum carefully with scissors. Punch a hole near the top with scissors.
4. Color with markers, and when dry, coat ornaments with shellac or nail polish.
5. When dry, run yarn through the hole in each ornament and tie loosely.

STAR BUNS

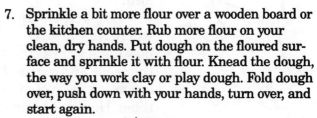

You need:
- Package of yeast (with an extra in reserve)
- 1/2 cup sugar
- 1/2 cup margarine
- 1 cup milk
- 1/4 teaspoon saffron, or 4 drops yellow food coloring
- 1/2 teaspoon salt
- 1 egg
- 4 cups, more or less, of enriched flour
- Oil for bowl and cookie sheet
- Wax paper to cover dough
- Golden raisins or slivered almonds

1. **Wash your hands first.** Run tap water on your wrist until it feels comfortable (not too warm or too cold). Put 1/4 cup of water this temperature into a bowl.
2. Add a package of yeast, and sprinkle 1/2 teaspoon of sugar over the yeast. Stir once, and let yeast dissolve.
3. Melt margarine in a pan, then add milk. Warm over low heat. (This mixture should feel like the water did on your wrist.) Remove from the stove, and stir in the salt and rest of the sugar. Crumble saffron into milk—or add yellow food coloring.
4. In a large bowl, break egg carefully (you might ask a grown-up to help). Beat egg with a fork or beater until fluffy. Add milk mixture to the egg.
5. Your yeast should be bubbly (you might even be able to hear it bubbling). But if not, try again with more yeast and water. (Yeast has to be fresh enough to raise the bread you are going to make.)
6. When yeast is bubbly, add it to eggs and milk. Mix carefully. Add about 3 cups of flour, one cup at a time, into the yeast mixture, mixing with a beater after each cup. When your dough begins to stretch, you can add a little more flour, mixing until dough is stiff. Dough should begin to stick together in a ball, and it will also stick to your hands. Wash your hands after you have used most of the flour.

7. Sprinkle a bit more flour over a wooden board or the kitchen counter. Rub more flour on your clean, dry hands. Put dough on the floured surface and sprinkle it with flour. Knead the dough, the way you work clay or play dough. Fold dough over, push down with your hands, turn over, and start again.

8. If dough begins to feel sticky while you knead it, add more flour, a little at a time to the dough and your hands. You know you have kneaded the dough enough when it looks and feels smooth and is no longer sticky.
9. Put the dough in an oiled bowl and cover with oiled wax paper. After you clean up the kitchen, you can rest, too, like the dough. (You should both be in a warm place, but not too hot—too much heat kills yeast.) The dough will take an hour or two to rise. (If you have something else to do, put dough in the refrigerator for a few hours, or even overnight.)

10. Wash and dry your hands again. Remove paper from bowl and punch down the dough to get rid of air bubbles. Knead again on a lightly floured board or counter. Preheat oven to 350 degrees. Pull off bits of dough about 2 inches thick. Roll into a ball, then flatten a little, making a circle.
11. Put buns on a greased cookie sheet about two inches apart. With a sharp knife, cut off pieces to make a "star". Sprinkle buns with raisins or almonds. Bake until puffed up and golden, about 25–30 minutes.

160

Keep the Birds Fat and Happy

In many countries in the Northern Hemisphere, winter is the cold season. What can happen when it gets cold? Lakes and ponds freeze. Snow falls, icicles form.

People spend more time inside their houses, where it's warm. Sometimes we forget that there are no worms or insects around for birds to eat. Many of the seeds and berries that were everywhere in the fall are now gone. We can help the birds out by feeding them. Here is a recipe they will love:

Bird Pudding

You need:
- 1 lb. of lard or leftover cooking fat
- 1 cup hot water
- 2 cups oatmeal
- 1 cup flour
- 4 cups wild birdseed

1. Warm the lard or fat in a frying pan.
2. Add the remaining ingredients and mix well with a spoon.
3. Put in bowls, or smear on tree trunks and pine cones while it is still soft.

BOWL FEEDER

1. With a hammer and nail, punch three holes evenly spaced along the rim of a plastic margarine tub.
2. Fill the tub with bird pudding.
3. Tie strings through the holes and hang the tub from a branch.

(Don't worry if the squirrels get to it. They are hungry, too.)

GOURMET CHRISTMAS TREE BIRD FEEDER

Once you're through with your Christmas tree, don't throw it away. Take it outside (still in the stand), and hang bird feeders from its branches.

- Smear bird pudding on the trunk.
- String popcorn and cranberries together and drape around the tree.
- Tie berry branches to the Christmas tree.
- Hang stale bread or doughnuts from the branches.

Mitten Match

Find the pairs of matching mittens. Draw
lines connecting the ones that are just alike.

Merry

___M I H S C A R T S___

Although we don't see much sunlight in December, this is many people's favorite month because of one very special day. It falls on the 25th. Do you know what it is? Fill in the crossword puzzle using the picture clues. Then unscramble the letters above to name this holiday.

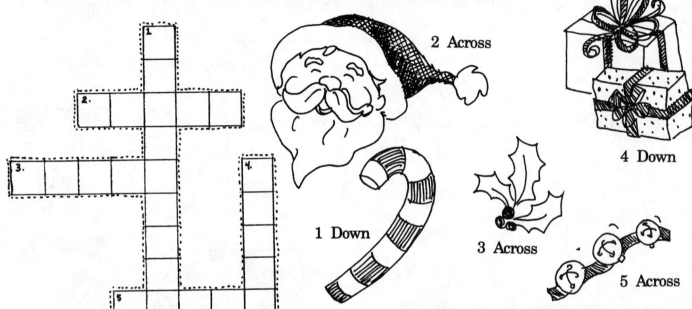

2 Across

4 Down

1 Down

3 Across

5 Across

For Christians, this is the happiest time of year. December 25 is the day Jesus Christ was born – almost 2,000 years ago.

On Christmas Eve, many Christians go to church. Others go on Christmas Day. They sing carols and pray that the world will be peaceful. And that people will be kind to each other.

Throughout the world, people celebrate this holy season with festivals. One night during the Christmas season, nearly every town in Mexico has a candle parade. The procession stops at every house, where the paraders sing carols and beg for a place to stay. When the hosts tell them they have no room, the paraders sing about how Joseph and Mary (Jesus' parents) needed shelter. Then the hosts invite the paraders into their homes. The children get to break a pinata filled with treats.

You know what happens on Christmas morning, don't you? It's time to give presents, just as the three wise men did when Jesus was born. Some people think it's a time to receive presents, but it's more fun to give than to receive, isn't it?

What's the first thing people say to each other on Christmas morning? "Merry Christmas." Here's how people in other countries say, "Merry Christmas":

England
"Happy Christmas"

Sweden
"God Jul"
(Goood Yule)

France
"Joyeux Noel"
(JWY-o No-EL)

Spain
"Felices Navidades"
(Fe-LEE-says Nav-i-DAD-ays)

Italy
"Buon Natale"
(Bwan Na-TA-lay)

A HOLIDAY REBUS
Based on the poem by Clement Moore
Color the Pictures that best complete this rebus.

T'was the 🌙 ☀ before 🎄 🎃 when all through the 🏚 🏠 ⛺, Not a creature was stirring, not even a 🐱 🐭 ; The 🧦 👢 👠 🍬 were hung by the 🔥 🏠 with care, In hopes that (fill in the dots!)

Soon would be there, Merry Christmas

Some Books To Read

P = preschoolers and up
K = kindergarten-aged children and up
E = elementary school students and up
J = mature elementary-school or junior-high students & up
A = all ages, even adults

How calendars work with the moon, stars, and sun:
UNDER THE SUN by Ellen Kandoian (New York: Dodd, Mead & Company, 1987) P
SUNSHINE MAKES THE SEASONS by Franklyn M. Branley, illustrated by Shelley Freshman (New York: Thomas Y. Crowell Let's-Read-And-Find-Out Science Books, 1974) K-E
SUN CALENDAR by Una Jacobs (Morristown, NJ: Silver Burdett Company, 1986) E-J
ANNO'S SUNDIAL by Mitsumasa Anno (New York: Philomel Books, 1985) A
THE BIG DIPPER and YOU by E. C. Krupp, illustrated by Robin Rector Krupp (New York: Morrow Junior Books, 1989) E-J
FIND THE CONSTELLATIONS by H. A. Rey, revised edition (Boston: Houghton Mifflin, 1976) A
THE SKY IS FULL OF STARS by Franklyn M. Branley, illustrated by Felicia Bond (New York: Thomas Y. Crowell, 1981) E

More holiday fun:
CELEBRATIONS by Myra Cohn Livingston and Leonard Everett Fisher (New York: Holiday House, 1985) A
PINATAS AND PAPER FLOWERS, Holidays of the Americas in English and Spanish by Lila Perl, illustrated by Victoria de Larrea, Spanish version by Alma Flor Ada (New York; Clarion Books, 1983) E
THE BOOK OF HOLIDAYS AROUND THE WORLD by Alice van Straalen (New York: E. P. Dutton, 1986) J
THE DAYS OF THE WEEK, Stories, songs, traditions, festivals, and surprising facts about the days of the week all over the world by Paul Hughes (London: Young Library Ltd., 1982 E (Also: THE MONTHS OF THE YEAR) E-J
I MADE IT MYSELF by Sabine Lohf (Chicago: Children's Press, 1990) E
MUDWORKS by MaryAnn Kohl, illustrated by Kathleen Kerr (Bellingham, WA: Bright Ring Publishing, 1989) A
LIGHT*THE*CANDLES!BEAT*THE*DRUMS! A book of Holidays, Occasions, Celebrations, Remembrances, Occurrences, Special Days, Weeks, and Months by Jane Sarnoff and Reynold Ruffins (New York: Charles Scribner's Sons, 1979) E-J

What's holy in holidays:
BIBLE STORIES FOR CHILDREN retold by Geoffrey Horn and Arthur Cavanaugh, illustrated by Arvis Stewart (New York: Macmillan Publishing Co., Inc., 1980) E
BOOK OF GREEK MYTHS by Ingri and Edgar Parin D'Aulaire (Garden City: Doubleday & Company, Inc., 1962) E
ISLAM by Christopher Barlow (London: B. T. Batsford, Ltd., 1983)
JEWISH HOLIDAY FUN by Judith Hoffman Corwin (New York: Messner Holiday Library/Simon & Schuster, Inc., 1987) E
NORSE GODS AND GIANTS by Ingri and Edgar Parin D'Aulaire (Garden City: Doubleday & Company, Inc., 1967) E
POWWOW by June Behrens (Chicago: Childrens Press, 1983) E
RELIGIONS OF THE WORLD by The Bookwright Press is a useful series that includes BUDDHISM, CHRISTIANITY, HINDUISM, JUDAISM, ISLAM, and SIKHISM E-J
SEASONS OF SPLENDOR, Tales, Myths & Legends of India by Madhur Jaffrey, Illustrated by Michael Foreman (New York: Atheneum, 1985) A
THE WORLD MYTHOLOGIES SERIES by Schocken Books includes North American Indian, Central and South American, Chinese, and Egyptian mythologies. J

Specific holidays:
THREE HAPPY BIRTHDAYS by Judith Caseley (New York: Greenwillow, 1989) P-E
EVERYONE HAS A BIRTHDAY by Caroline Arnold, illustrated by Anthony Accardo (New York: Franklin Watts, 1987) E
CANDLES, CAKES, AND DONKEY TAILS, Birthday Symbols and Celebrations by Lila Perls, illustrations by Victoria de Larrea (New York: Clarion Books, 1984) E-J

WHO FOUND AMERICA? by Johanna Johnston (Chicago: Children's Press, 1973) P
I, COLUMBUS by Lisa Weil (New York: Atheneum, 1983) E
WHERE DO YOU THINK YOU'RE GOING, CHRISTOPHER COLUMBUS? by Jean Fritz (New York: Putnam, 1980) J
LEIF ERIKSON THE LUCKY by Malcom C. Jensen (New York: Franklin Watts, 1979) J

CHRISTMAS GIFT-BRINGERS by Leonard B. Lubin (New York: William Morrow & Company, 1989) A

TAKE JOY! The Tasha Tudor Christmas Book, selected, edited and illustrated by Tasha Tudor (New York: Philomel Books, 1966) A

THE RAFFI CHRISTMAS TREASURY, Fourteen Illustrated Songs and Musical Arrangements, illustrated by Nadine Bernard Westcott (New York: Crown Publishers, Inc., 1988) P-E

MERRY CHRISTMAS, Children at Christmastime Around the World by Satomi Ichikawa with text by Robina Beckles Willson (New York: Philomel Books, 1983) K-E

THE TRUTH ABOUT SANTA CLAUS by James Cross Giblin (New York: Thomas Y. Crowell, 1985) J

APRIL FOOLS' DAY by Emily Kelley (Minneapolis: Carol Rhoda Books, 1983) E

MY FIRST EASTER BOOK by Annetta E. Dellinger, illustrated by Linda Hohag (Chicago: Childrens Press, 1985) P

THE STORY OF THE EASTER BUNNY by Sheila Black, illustrated by Robyn Officer (New York: Golden Books, 1988) P-E

LILIES, RABBITS, AND PAINTED EGGS, The Story of Easter Symbols by Edna Barth, illustrated by Ursula Arndt (New York: Houghton Mifflin/Clarion Books, 1970) E-J

MY FIRST HANUKKAH BOOK by Aileen Fisher (Chicago: Childrens Press, 1985) P-E

ALL ABOUT HANUKKAH by Judye Groner and Madeline Wikler, illustrated by Rosalyn Schanzer (Rockville, MD: Kar-Ben Copies, Inc., 1988) K-E

HANUKKAH, Eight Nights, Eight Lights by Malka Druker, drawings by Brom Hoban (New York: Holiday House, 1980) J

THE POWER OF LIGHT by Isaac B. Singer (New York: Farrar, Straus & Giroux, 1980) A

HAPPY HALLOWEEN! Costumes & Masks to Make Yourself, Riddles*Recipes*Magic, Plus Much More by Phyllis Hoffman, illustrated by Tom Hoffman (New York, Atheneum, 1982) E

HIST WHIST by e.e. cummings, illustrated by Deborah Kogan Ray (New York: Crown Publishers, Inc., 1989) A

THE PENNYWHISTLE HALLOWEEN BOOK by Meredith Brokaw and Annie Gilbar, illustrated by Jill Weber (New York: Weidenfeld & Nicolson, 1989) E-J

THE STAR-SPANGLED BANNER, by Francis Scott Key, illustrated by Peter Spier (New York: Doubleday & Company, Inc., 1973) A

FIREWORKS, PICNICS, AND FLAGS, The Story of the Fourth of July Symbols by James Cross Giblin, illustrated by Ursula Arndt (New York: Clarion Books, 1983) J

MARTIN LUTHER KING, JR., Free at Last by David A. Adler, illustrated by Robert Casilla (New York: Holiday House, 1986) E

THE GREAT AMERICANS SERIES, Martin Luther King, Jr. by Kathie Billingslea Smith, illustrated by James Seward (New York: Julian Messner, 1987) E

MARCHING TO FREEDOM, The Story of Martin Luther King, Jr. by Joyce Milton (New York: Dell Yearling Books, 1987) E-J

MEMORIAL DAY by Geoffrey Scott, pictures by Peter E. Hanson (Minneapolis: Carol Rhoda On My Own Books, 1983) E

HAPPY NEW YEAR by Emily Kelley, pictures by Priscilla Kiedrowski (Minneapolis: Carol Rhoda On My Own Books, 1984) E

A PICTURE BOOK OF PASSOVER by David A. Adler, illustrated by Linda Heller (New York: Holiday House, 1982) K-E

PASSOVER by June Behrens, photos by Terry Behrens (Chicago: Childrens Press, 1987) E

THE STORY OF GEORGE WASHINGTON by May McNeer, pictures by Lynd Ward (Nashville: Abington Press, 1973) E

WORLD LEADERS PAST & PRESENT, George Washington by Roger Bruns (New York: Chelsea House Publishers, 1987) J

ABRAHAM LINCOLN by Ingri & Edgar Pari D'Aulaire (Garden City: Doubleday & Company, 1957) K-E

CHILDHOOD OF FAMOUS AMERICANS: Abraham Lincoln, The Great Emancipator by Augusta Stevenson, illustrated by Jerry Robinson (New York: Aladdin Books, 1959) E

ME AND WILLIE AND PA, The Story of Abraham Lincoln and his son Tad by F.N. Monjo, illustrated by Douglas Gorsline (New York: Simon and Schuster, 1973) E-J

ESTHER by Miriam Chaikin, illustrated by Vera Rosenberry (Philadelphia: The Jewish Publication Society, 1987) E

HADASSAH, Esther, the Orphan Queen by William H. Armstrong, illustrated by Barbara Byfield (Garden City, NJ: Doubleday & Co., Inc., c. 1972) J

PURIM by Molly Cone, illustrated by Helen Borten (Toronto: Crowell Holiday Book, 1967) A

SOUND THE SHOFAR, The Story and Meaning of Rosh Hashanah and Yom Kippur by Miriam Chaikin, illustrated by Erika Weihs (New York: Clarion Books, 1986) E-J

OUR ST. PATRICK'S DAY BOOK by Sandra Ziegler, illustrated by Gwen Connelly (Chicago: Childrens Press, 1987) P-E

ST. PATRICK'S DAY by Mary Cantwell, illustrated by Usrula Arndt (New York: Thomas Y. Crowell Company, 1967) E-J

MY FIRST THANKSGIVING BOOK by Jane Belk Moncure, illustrated by Gwen Connelly (Chicago: Childrens Press, 1984) P-E

THANKSGIVING, A First Book, By Margaret Baldwin (New York: Franklin Watts, 1983) E-J

THE THANKSGIVING BOOK by Frank Jupo (New York: Dodd, Mead & Co., 1980) J

OVER THE RIVER and THROUGH THE WOOD by Lydia Maria Child, illustrated by Brinton Turkle (New York: Coward, McCann & Geoghegan, Inc., 1974) A

THINGS TO MAKE AND DO FOR VALENTINE'S DAY by Tomie De Paola (New York: Franklin Watts, 1976) P-E

IT'S VALENTINE'S DAY by Jack Prelutsky, illustrated by Yossi Abolafia (New York: Greenwillow Read-Aloud Books, 1983) K-E

VALENTINE'S DAY, A First Book by Fern G. Brown (New York: Franklin Watts, 1983) J

ANSWERS

Page 1. A burning candle can help tell that time has passed, but is not really a "timepiece." Neither the moon, nor a sundial is very exact – you can't tell time with them if it's cloudy, can you? The calendar, clock, hourglass, and watch ARE all excellent timepieces.

Page 4. Building snowmen and bundling up against the cold are winter-time activities in the Northern Hemisphere, when the earth tilts away (A) from the sun. Swimming and eating ice cream are summer-time activities north of the Equator, when the earth tilts toward the sun (T) again.

Page 5. The US and Canada are in the top part of earth, or the Northern Hemisphere.

Page 6. January = Snow Moon; February = Hunger Moon; March = Crow Moon; April = Green Grass Moon; May = Planting Moon; June = Rose Moon; July = Thunder Moon; August = Green Corn Moon; September = Hunting Moon; October = Falling Leaf Moon; November = Mad (Crazy) Moon; December = Long Night Moon.

Page 7. There are 12 months in a year. When you multiply 29.5 times 12, you get 354, but a year is really 365 days long. The difference between moon and sun time is 11 days each year, so after a few years of using calendars, people found their dates and seasons were wrong.

Page 9. January, March, May, July, August, October, and December are each 31 days long.

Page 10. Half of December, all of January and February, and half of March should be colored blue. Half of March, all of April and May, and half of June should be yellow. Did you color half of June, all of July and August, and half of September green? Half of September, all of October and November, and half of December are fall. Did you color them red?

Page 43. Orange Bowl = Miami, FL; Rose Bowl = Pasadena, CA; Fiesta Bowl = Tempe, AZ; Cotton Bowl = Dallas, TX; Sugar Bowl = New Orleans, LA.

Who won the game? The point spread was 1.

Knee Knockers:		Crushers:	
3 touchdowns	18	2 touchdowns	12
2 extra points	2	2 extra points	2
3 field goals	9	4 field goals	12
1 safety	2	2 safeties	4
	31		30

Page 48. The Chinese "invented" paper, the noodle, the clock, the calculator (theirs is called an abacus), and the rocket.

Page 49. The Chinese name each year after an animal: rat, ox, tiger, rabbit, dragon, snake, horse, sheep, monkey, rooster, dog, pig. 1993 is the year of the rooster, 1999 is the year of the rabbit. The horse comes back in 2002.

Page 50. 1 down: Valentine; 1 across: violets; 2 across: purple; 3 across: true; 4 across: Honest.

Page 51. If you were born on February 29, 1984, you have had only one birthday by 1990, but you would be six years old! Did you find a foot, faucet, five, four, flag, fireman, finger, flashlight, fur, fez, flame, football, fish, fork, fan, flute, frankfurter in frankfurter bun, fox, fence, flower, and flyswatter in Mr. Frog's Mouth. The fly is not (yet) inside.

Page 52.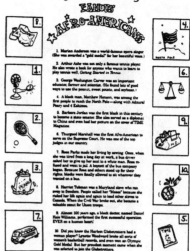

Page 54. Rebus Valentine messages: I love you, Please Be Mine, My Heart Beats For You, Too Cute To Be Forgotten.

Page 55. Candy, hearts, and cupid are all signs of this holiday.

Page 56. Abraham Lincoln learned to write with a buzzard's feather, freed the slaves, and was known as "Honest Abe." George Washington grew up on a plantation in Virginia and is still remembered as the "Father of his Country."

Page 57.

Page 58. The second and fifth masks from the left are exactly alike.

Page 60. We made 50 words from festival, without any plurals: ail, ale, at, ate, east, eat, evil, fail, fast, fate, feast, feat, felt, fiesta, file, fit, five, flat, if, is, it, last, late, leaf, least, lift, live, safe, sail, sale, save, seal, seat, sift, silt, sit, slave, stale, stave, steal, stile, tale, teal, tail, tile, vale, veal, vile, vital, vista.

Page 63. The wind surfer, anemometer (a device that measures wind), bubble-maker, kite, windmill, wind sock, flag and sailboat all need wind.

Page 68.

168

Page 69. Shamrocks are green.

Page 70. Did you find the flower with 7 petals? We counted 31 insects the hungry plants could eat.

Page 72. The flower, door, envelope, box, window, satchel, bottle, and egg all can open (or be opened).

Page 73.

Page 74.

Page 75.

Page 77. We counted 25 raindrops (big and little) but couldn't agree on the number of tiny drops within drops.

Page 78. 40 Easter eggs, including the one just hatched.

Page 79. The Aleutian Islands, in the State of Alaska, would be the last place in the US where Americans see the Easter sun rise.

Page 80.

Page 82.

Page 90.

Page 91. Carol Leach wrapped up a bag of flour, a pound of butter, a wine glass, teapot, boot, cow, pig, and umbrella.

Page 92. 37 states have joined the Union, making a total of 50 stars on today's US flag.

Page 93. HAPPY FLAG DAY. A white flag means, "Surrender." You might see the black and white check flag at the Indianapolis 500 auto races on Memorial Day.

Page 94. Human, deer, sheep, goose, and horse "Dads."

Page 95. Sandra Day O'Connor, Martin Luther King, Esther, Neil Armstrong.

Page 96. There are 92 days or three months in summer. Celery = stem; carrot = root; broccoli = bud; tomato = fruit; spinach = leaf; potato = tuber; pea = seed.

Page 97. We "hooked" a bathing suit, several fish, a flyswatter, mosquito, sand castle, ice cream cone, lightning bolt, sandal, sailboat, "no school" sign, snake, shell, seaweed, weeds, snail, suntan lotion, bugs, sunglasses, flower, fan.

Page 100. There are 21 soccer balls, two different from the rest.

Page 101.

169

Page 102.

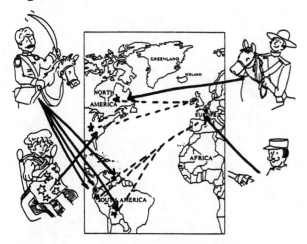

Page 103. Robert Livingston didn't sign.

Page 104. We think Neil Armstrong's footprint is still on the moon. Do you?

Page 105. We counted three 0's; 24 1's; three 2's, 3's, 4's, 5's; five 6's and 7's; eleven 8's, and two 9's.

Page 106. States you visit more than once, color orange. Iowa to Florida = 1200 miles; Montana to Michigan = 1350 miles; California to Massachusetts with stops along the way = 3600 miles.

Page 109.

Page 110.

Page 111.

Page 112-3. Did you find this clown's twin?

Page 115.

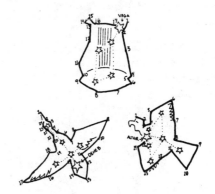

Page 116. We found several rings, a whistle, ball, scissors, animal, rabbit's foot, thimble, die, and coin hidden in the birthday cake.

Page 118.

Page 119. Apples, asparagus, avocados, eggplant, olives, oranges, and yams begin with vowels.

Page 120. CARPENTER; TENNIS PRO; ARTIST; MINER; MUSICIAN; POSTAL WORKER; CLOWN; DANCER; NURSE; ASTRONAUT

Page 121.

Page 123. We counted 30 monarch butterflies, including a caterpillar and a cocoon.

Page 126.

Page 127. We found 24 words from the letters in neighbor: be, begin, big, bone, brine, bore, born, go, gone, gore, grin, he, hen, her, hog, horn, no, nor, neigh, or, reign, rig, rob, robe.

Page 129.

Page 130.

Page 132. October is the 10th month.

Page 133. Mrs. Squirrel has 27 nuts stored up for winter, and we counted that many in the picture.

Page 134. Santa Maria.

Page 136. 1. USSR 2. The United States 3. Australia 4. Brazil 5. India 6. Canada 7. Spain 8. Egypt 9. Japan 10. China.

Page 137.

Page 138. Halloween is October 31st.

Page 139.

Page 140. Three teddy bears, five balls, and seven gifts.

Page 144.

Page 145. We counted 5 votes for the Democrat, Mrs. Jones, and 7 for the Republican candidate, Mr. Smith.

Page 146. Sailor = protect our seas; Soldier = national defense; Marine = guard embassies; Pilot = newest branch of armed forces; Coast Guardsman = helps boaters.

Navy 1   Army 2   Marines 3   Air Force 4   Coast Guard 5

Page 149. Madeleine L'Engle wrote *Meet the Austins* and *A Wrinkle in Time*. *Green Eggs and Ham* and *The Sneeches* are by Dr. Seuss. *Chicken Soup with Rice* and *Where the Wild Things Are* are Maurice Sendak's work.

Page 150. Aunt, uncle, niece, nephew, cousin.

Page 151. Turkey.

Page 152. December is the 12th (and last) month of the year. In Australia, in the Southern Hemisphere, the first day of winter is a long day.

Page 153.

Page 154. Menorahs (left to right): seventh, third, fifth, second, and fourth nights of Hanukkah.

Page 157. We counted 57 (some very tiny) stars in all the pictures, before you drew yours.

Page 161.

Page 162. Christmas. 1 down: candy cane; 1 across: Santa; 3 across: holly; 4 down: gifts; 5 across: bells.

Page 163.

Other books by Ed and Roon Frost:

COAST GUIDE: Seabrook, NH to Freeport, ME.
Scenic routes by car, bike, and foot for travelers and
natives with information on beaches, boat trips,
historic sites, shopping, restaurants, nature areas,
attractions for children. $9.95
ISBN 0-9618806-0-0

Says Charles Gibson of ABC's "Good Morning, America":
   "INCREDIBLE! Imagine putting an entire 80 miles of
coastline right in your glove compartment. . . The Frosts'
book is a practical guide to a pretty area and will give you
everything from the best local lore to lobster lunch
locations."
   ". . .one of the most **useful** travel guides I've seen —
logical and well-organized. . . full of the quirky bits of
history. . . that add much to the pleasure of a place."
Frances Carnahan, Editor, EARLY AMERICAN LIFE.

**Recommended by
BOSTON, FRIENDS, and TOURING MAGAZINES.**

*MOUNTAIN GUIDE: The White Mountains of New
Hampshire and Maine.* The first complete four-
seasons guide for car, bike, and foot, with maps and
information on skiing (cross-country and downhill),
fishing, shopping, hiking, local lore and more. $9.95
ISBN 0-9618806-1-9

   "The maps, drawings, quotations, anecdotes, personal
observations, and deft brushstrokes make it useful and
entertaining for those exploring western Maine and the
White Mountains." DOWNEAST.

   "Even if you never plan to slip into a pair of hiking
boots, don a pair of skis, or wet a line, this book is. . .
the most useful and least complex guide to anywhere that
I've ever seen."
Hale G. Joy, THE ELLSWORTH AMERICAN.

**Recommended by
The Appalachian Mountain Club, CAMPERWAYS,
and NORTHEAST OUTDOORS.**

And with Carol Leach, "who is either a kid or
has a perfect memory":
*JUST FOR KIDS: The New England Guide &
Activity Book.* Just right for kids over five: includes
stories, time-line, puzzles, nature guides, coloring
pages, connect-the-dots, mazes, codes, postcards to
color and send, places for families to visit. $7.95
ISBN 0-9618806-2-7

   "Full of games, pictures, suggestions and other
marvels, this book is a boon to both kids and parents, who
ought to make it a best seller. Get one. Get several."
Marilis Hornidge, BOOK BAG REVIEWS.

**Recommended by
ENDLESS VACATION, FAMILY CIRCLE,
and PARENTS' MAGAZINES.**

If not available in a bookstore near you, contact:
   Independent Publishers Group
   814 North Franklin Street
   Chicago, IL 60610
   1-800/888-4741
Please include $3 for postage and handling.